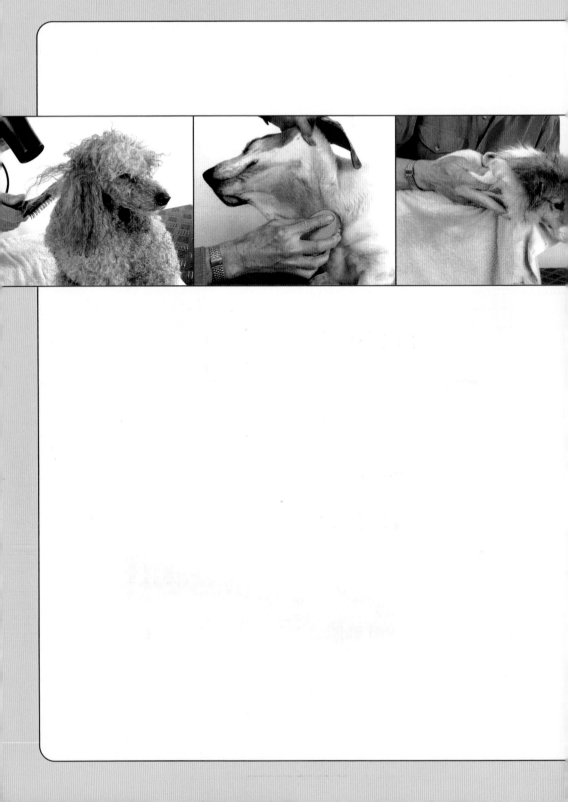

GROOMING YOUR DOG

Top professional tips and expert advice to ensure the best in home grooming

PETER YOUNG

INTERPET PUBLISHING

Published by
Interpet Publishing,
Vincent Lane,
Dorking,
Surrey RH4 3YX,
England

ISBN 978-1-84286-220-9

The recommendations in this
book are given without any
guarantees on the part of the
author and publisher. If in
doubt, seek the advice of a
vet or pet-care specialist.

Credits
Editor: Philip de Ste. Croix
Designer: Philip Clucas
Diagram artwork: Martin Reed
Photography: Mark Burch
Production management:
    Consortium, Suffolk
Print production: 1010
    Printworks International Ltd,
    Hong Kong
Printed and bound in China

Credits
The author would like to
express his grateful thanks
to Anita Bax, Shaun Thorpe,
and the owners who kindly
brought in their dogs for
photography: Iris Cox and
Ricky, Tracy Edney and Rosie
and Chilli, Linda Whitehouse
and Tilly, Beverley Cuddy and
Oscar, Mr Roberts and Billy,
and Mr Spink and Flo.

Peter Young is an
internationally
renowned
poodle breeder,
handler and
Crufts-accredited
judge. He has
made up around
20 champions in different breeds.
Peter is also one of the grooming
world's celebrities. Owner of Peter's
Posh Pets, a grooming parlour
located in West London, he holds
many grooming contest titles, among
them "Intergroom International
Groomer of the Year", one of the
most prestigious awards in the world
of grooming. He has won six gold
medals on behalf of the UK at
international grooming competitions.
He has also judged many grooming
competitions around the world,
including "Intergroom International
Groomer of the Year". Peter has won
three Cardinal Crystal Achievement
Awards, the Oscars of the grooming
industry: two for "International
Groomer of the Year" and one for
"Grooming Contest Judge of the
Year". Peter co-organises the
Eurogroom annual competition
and teaching event with the help
of fellow groomer and poodle
breeder Anita Bax.

CONTENTS

PART ONE

• The first section explains why we need to groom dogs, looking at the structure and purpose of hair and skin, the seasonal variations in coat density that dogs experience, and recommending where and how to start grooming at home. **8-13**

• The condition of a dog's coat is affected by external factors, like allergies and parasites, as well diet, general health, age and weather conditions. This section advises on how to maintain a coat in the optimum condition. **14-29**

• Good grooming practice extends beyond simply looking after the dog's coat. A responsible owner will also need to make regular checks of eyes, ears, teeth and nails and follow the routines described to maintain good physical condition. **30-37**

• There is an abundance of grooming products on the market, from different types of brushes and combs to many varieties of shampoo and conditioner. Here the author gives guidance on the essential kit that a home groomer will need. **38-43**

Caring For Your Dog

Caring for your pet is so important. It really is an essential part of dog ownership, and it does not have to be chore. Small amounts of regular care and attention can make such a lot of difference to both your lives.

Many owners fall into the trap of allowing their pets to develop bad habits, and this applies to grooming and coat maintenance as much as it does to behaviour. I hope the guidance given here with regard to grooming will help you to avoid the pitfalls that you can easily fall into when caring for a dog. The whole basis of pet owning is that it should bring joy to your life. And – a little like rearing children – it is your responsibility to educate and care for your pet. It doesn't work the other way round!

I hope that this book helps your dog to enjoy the love and sense of physical well-being that it deserves. This first section shows why dog owners should understand the need for grooming, and describes the nature of dogs' skin and hair, and how we can best look after them.

WHAT IS HAIR?

Hair is a horny, flexible, elastic filament. The length, diameter and texture of hair vary, as does its form (straight, wavy or curly). All hair is made up from keratin, a tough, fibrous protein which is the same ingredient that is found in nails, claws and horns, but in a much more compacted form. Hairs grow from follicles that are found all over the body in the dermal layer of the skin. Except for a few growing cells at the base of the root, the shaft of the hair that is visible above the skin is dead tissue, composed of keratin and related proteins.

● There are three main stages in the development of each hair. First you have the anagen (growth) stage, which is the initial period of growth when the bulb of the hair root is very firmly attached to the follicle. The average time a hair spends in this stage is around 100 days but in very long coated breeds it can last up to 550 days.

● Following this comes the catagen (intermediate) phase when most of the hair is grown and the follicle goes into a resting mode and the hair bulb gradually disorganises itself.

● Finally there comes the telogen (dormancy) phase, when the hair is anchored by only a few keratin roots. The base of the hair shrinks to a cone shape and the individual hair eventually

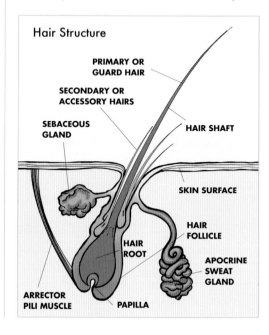

Hair Structure

PRIMARY OR GUARD HAIR

SECONDARY OR ACCESSORY HAIRS

SEBACEOUS GLAND

HAIR SHAFT

SKIN SURFACE

HAIR FOLLICLE

HAIR ROOT

APOCRINE SWEAT GLAND

ARRECTOR PILI MUSCLE

PAPILLA

the poodle, Afghan, Maltese etc. This type is a little more like human hair; they do still moult but not until the hair shaft is extremely long. In this way the moulting is less noticeable, as explained above in relation to the growth time in the anagen stage.

HAIR – WHAT IS ITS PURPOSE?

The principle purpose of a dog's coat is to protect the animal from the elements. For example, a thick coat protects against extreme cold. Huskies in the snow, for instance, have a very thick, dense double coat which traps air to provide a protective layer of insulation to keep the animals warm. This layer of air also helps to keep them cool in summer. Another type of coat guards against extreme heat and strong sun, such as that of Pharaoh Hounds which have very fine coats. For all the water retrieving breeds a double coat with a thick, oily, waterproof outer layer is necessary to stop the dog from becoming saturated with water when it is swimming. Again, the air trapped between the dense undercoat and the outer coat acts as an insulator to help keep the animals warm in the sometimes very cold waters in which they work.

So, the type of coat usually reflects the dog's original native environment. Nature in its wonderful way has developed hair and coat patterns that are the optimum adaptations to protect the dog from the climatic extremes that it may experience.

Above: *Grooming your dog can be a pleasure, not a chore. You get to spend quality time with your pet who will value this token of your care.*

falls out. Another hair then begins to grow, starting with the anagen phase and growing in the same follicle as its predecessor.

• Hair basically falls into two categories. First, there are moulting hairs. These are affected by the seasonal weather conditions, i.e. a dog loses its winter coat in preparation for a warm summer, and then sheds the summer coat to prepare for a warmer, thicker winter one. These coats grow to short to medium length, and the majority of breeds have coats of this type. There are also continuously growing hairs like those found on

Caring For Your Dog

SKIN – WHAT IS ITS PURPOSE?

Briefly, the essential purpose of the skin is to cover the body and protect the underlying tissues and organs. It is, in fact, the largest organ in the body. It is also responsible for conveying information about the animal's environment, such as temperature, and the objects with which it comes into contact through the nerves that are present in the skin. The skin is sensitive to touch and pain and will warn the animal of any danger from sharp objects etc.

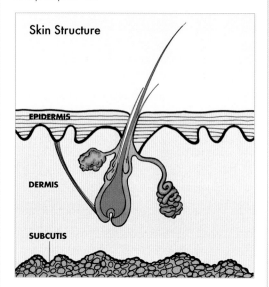

Skin Structure

EPIDERMIS

DERMIS

SUBCUTIS

The skin is a keratinous structure of three layers. The epidermis is the top or outer layer. It forms a tough, waterproof barrier and serves as a protective layer. It is continually in the process of flaking off – dead surface cells are shed while they are replenished from the constant supply of new cells being formed at a lower level of the dermis. These cells then migrate to the surface to form the epidermis. This process keeps the surface layer in perfect, healthy condition and repairs damage to the skin caused by injury. The length of time it takes the cells formed in the dermis to reach the surface is around 20 days.

Below this lies the dermis. This is a tough, flexible layer which is where the hair follicles are formed and rooted, before extending outwards through the epidermis. In dogs a number of hairs group together to emerge through a common opening. One hair in such a group is often thicker and longer than the others and is called a guard hair. The rest of the coat is formed by the smaller, softer hairs in the bunch. The size of these bunches will vary according to the coat type. The dermis contains the elastic fibres and collagen that give the skin its toughness and pliability, as well as the nerves and erector muscles which enable the dog to react to pain and touch. The erector muscle also has the ability to adjust the lie of the hair so that the dog can display its reaction to other dogs by making itself look bigger and raising its hackles if needed.

Below the dermis comes the subcutis, which is really just a subcutaneous fat layer. Only the dermis and the subcutis contain blood vessels and nerves.

The protective layers of the skin bear thick outer guard hairs and smaller, soft accessory hairs which provide good insulation from the cold. Glandular secretions (sebum), which are made in the sebaceous glands situated in the dermis, add shine to the coat and make it waterproof. They also play a protective role by destroying bacteria on the skin surface.

GROOMING – WHAT IS ITS PURPOSE ?

When a number of animals gather together in a group, grooming often performs the function of a social exercise, either between pairs of animals or in a wider social context as part of a group. This interactive grooming has two functions: firstly, it is important for coat maintenance, and secondly it helps to establish and/or maintain a hierarchy of status within the group or pair. When this activity is transferred to our domestic environment, you and your dog(s) are involved in a new type of relationship – you have to exercise a form of silent control by deed rather than spoken command (which dogs sometime choose not to hear!).

The purpose of mutual grooming in the wild is to check for parasites and make sure that the coat is free from debris. In a way, this is not so dissimilar to the reasons why we choose to groom our pets: we want to keep the coat clean and tangle-free. In the wild, dogs rely on their coats to protect them from the elements, and the many different regions in which the dog was, or still is, native and the environments in which it developed have given rise to the many different types of coats we have today – along with a little creative interference from man!

Some of these dogs grew and bred in climates which experienced great seasonal variations – they were very cold in winter and warm in summer. Over time, many dogs (as well as a lot of other animals) have developed a distinct winter coat and a lighter summer coat. In order to produce a new coat, the dog needs to shed the previous one. In many hairy breeds that have been domesticated, this is where problems can arise. If the older coat does not free itself and fall away cleanly from the new growth, clumping, matting and tangling occurs.

Nowadays a lot of breeds have even thicker and denser coats than would be the case in the wild. This development has been brought about by selective breeding, and it means that more grooming and maintenance is required, and owners must be prepared for this as the dogs cannot manage effective coat management on their own. Originally, dogs would have shed the previous coat, once the process of moulting had started, by rolling on sand or on grass, or by rubbing up against bushes, hedges or rocks to help free them of the loose hair. Now, when they want to do this, the object of their attentions is more likely to be our carpets and sofas! This is another reason why it makes sense to learn how to groom your dog routinely at home.

Left: *For puppies licking, play biting and mutual grooming is all part of the learning experience.*

11

Caring For Your Dog

WHERE AND HOW TO GROOM

It is worth taking some time to consider where will be the best and most convenient place to groom your dog. You want to make a well-informed decision as your comfort while grooming should be a very important part in developing your sense of enjoyment and bonding with your pet.

There are several reasons why you should have an area that you use specifically for grooming. Ideally, you should use a table – or worktop – which is stable and of a good height for you (either sitting or standing) onto which you can put your dog. Somewhere perhaps in a garage, utility room, workshop or kitchen. Make sure the chosen location has a non-slip surface so as to make your pet feel safe. A couple of rubber car mats laid on a slippery surface will often suffice. The psychology behind this is that by lifting your dog up from the floor, which it will regard as its own domain, and standing it on a table, you are transferring it into your domain and

quietly asserting your authority over it. The pet will realise that it is now in your personal workspace and it should have more regard for you as a result. Also, as it is confined to a smaller area and lifted up off the ground, your dog cannot run off and hide behind the sofa, escape upstairs or flee out into the garden with you in hot pursuit.

The grooming session should not be seen as a play event, and it should be conducted as a serious time when you concentrate on your pet, with a play and reward session afterwards. It is very easy to start play-grooming with a puppy, letting it chew the brush etc., but as the dog gets older, it becomes extremely hard to break them of this habit. It is much better not to let them begin playing around during grooming in the first place.

Starting To Groom A Puppy

It is best to start with very short grooming sessions when your puppy is young and might not even look as if it needs grooming. Put the youngster onto the table and lightly brush him. Check inside his ears and look at his mouth, check his feet, and perhaps bathe his eyes. Also make sure he has a clean rear end daily or at least two or three times a week (finish with a little play or a reward afterwards). This routine establishes that this is serious time between owner and pet. And it keeps you aware of the pup's physical condition.

If your puppy is very wriggly or you are just starting to groom an older dog, perhaps see if

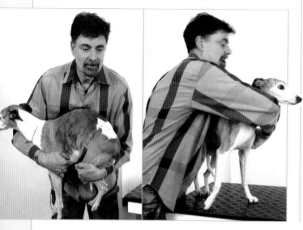

Both left: *By lifting your dog up onto a special grooming station, you establish that grooming is not a time for play, but a serious activity when you will assert gentle but firm authority over the dog for a period that you will determine.*

The Language of Grooming

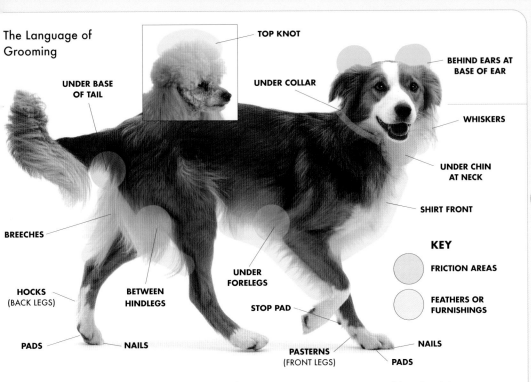

TOP KNOT

UNDER BASE
OF TAIL

UNDER COLLAR

BEHIND EARS AT
BASE OF EAR

WHISKERS

UNDER CHIN
AT NECK

SHIRT FRONT

BREECHES

UNDER
FORELEGS

KEY

FRICTION AREAS

HOCKS
(BACK LEGS)

BETWEEN
HINDLEGS

STOP PAD

FEATHERS OR
FURNISHINGS

PADS

NAILS

PASTERNS
(FRONT LEGS)

NAILS

PADS

Above: *The annotations pinpoint some special terms that you will find in this book. It is important to groom friction areas thoroughly as the coat here has a natural tendency to mat and tangle.*

you can get another member of the household to help you initially by holding the pet still. This is best done by putting on the dog's collar and getting the helper to stand in front of the pet and to hold the collar gently at each side of the dog's head, thus restricting head movement. This is reassuring and comforting for the dog and enables the groomer to progress more quickly .

If you are on your own and do not have the benefit of help, again put a collar on the pet, but this time also attach a lead. If possible, position the grooming table against a wall, near a hook or something to which you can attach the lead to keep the dog's head under control (much as when you see a horse tethered for grooming in a stable yard). In a way, tethering a dog like this almost

gives you an extra pair of hands while restricting the movement of the pet. However, never leave a tethered dog unattended on the table as, if it were to jump off, it could be disastrous. Keep the lead quite taut to avoid this happening.

Once the dog is mature and puppy tangles have gone, and depending on the thickness and texture of mature coat, grooming can become a daily routine if time and aptitude allow. You should try to do it two or three times a week and certainly a full, thorough grooming should be carried out at least once a week. It is better to groom thoroughly once a week covering every area scrupulously rather than simply tickling the coat with a brush every other day for days on end, but not getting to the base of the hair shafts and thereby letting mats and tangles form.

Dogs will often enjoy a grooming session with their owner very much as the dog has the uninterrupted, devoted attention of their owner for however long the session takes.

Maintaining A Healthy Coat

THE EFFECT OF YOUR DOG'S GENERAL HEALTH ON ITS COAT

As with humans, a dog's levels of health and fitness are reflected in its appearance. If you provide the correct amount of quality food and fresh water and ensure that the dog enjoys proper exercise, you should be the owner of a dog that is in good shape and possessing a healthy skin and coat.

Obesity in pets (as below) is a condition that can develop very easily, and especially in neutered animals. It can cause or aggravate other disorders, such as diabetes and some of the endocrine diseases such as Cushing's disease which is caused by excess production of a hormone from the adrenal gland. This can lead to hair loss and skin lesions. Obesity may also contribute to serious skin problems, which will have a detrimental effect on the coat quality and its density. Overweight dogs always moult a lot more than dogs which have the correct body weight for their size.

Feeding dogs on an unhealthy diet will reflect in a poor quality, lack-lustre coat. It must be stressed that the provision of a good, well-balanced diet is essential for a healthy coat and well-conditioned skin.

As well as allowing a dog to eat its food efficiently, maintenance of good dental hygiene is also essential for a dog's well-being as decaying teeth and progressive gum disease slowly but surely poison the dog's system.

DIET AND ITS EFFECTS ON THE COAT

What you feed a dog has a great deal of influence on your pet's growth, development and condition. A nutritious, well-balanced diet in suitable quantities helps to produce a well-muscled, healthily coated and happy dog. There are so many different ways in which you can feed your dog, with a huge range of commonly produced products to choose from. It will pay you to take some time to research the diet that will best suit your dog. Talk to your vet if you feel you need more advice.

Dogs are not true carnivores and cannot exist on meat alone, unlike cats. Meat, which provides protein, should not form more than half of their diet. The rest of the daily calories should come from carbohydrates, which can be found in dog meal and/or vegetables including raw carrots, cabbage, raw or cooked potatoes. Dogs love apples, too! Protein is needed for growth, tissue repair and maintenance of metabolic processes. Essential fatty acids give a glossy shine to a dog's coat and help to maintain a healthy skin. Carbohydrates add bulk to the diet and help maintain regular bowel movement. A balanced diet – be it a commercially made complete food or one prepared by yourself – should have all the vitamins and bulk your pet requires.

Daily requirements vary, depending on what sort of breed you have, your dog's activity levels and what stage in its life it has reached. During puppyhood and the growing stages of any breed, frequent meals throughout the day of a high quality food, with added vitamins and minerals and sufficient calories, help to maintain a good growth pattern. If you are feeding a complete food, adequate vitamins and minerals should already be included in the mix, but if it's your own dietary plan these supplements, readily available in pet stores, should be added. At the other end of the scale, senior dogs require far fewer calories as their energy demands drop quite significantly. Of course, very active types of dog require a higher intake of food than less active types to maintain

Above: *An apple is a healthy treat that most dogs will enjoy.*

optimum levels of condition. But a good, balanced diet provided in correct amounts combined with regular, ample exercise should ensure that your dog will have a healthy coat and skin. If the dog is in good condition generally, this will be reflected in its coat, which will possibly demand less attention. Improperly fed dogs often have dull coats and seem listless by comparison.

Dogs which are overweight will generally shed or moult a lot more than dogs of an appropriate weight (see the advice on moulting and how to deal with it on pages 28-29), and they also feel the heat a lot more. Neutering can also cause dogs easily to get overweight, and it will often also affect their hair growth pattern (see pages 24-25).

Making sure that your dog is free from internal parasites (i.e. by regular worming) also helps to ensure your pet is deriving the maximum benefit from its food (see pages 18-23 for information about dealing with parasites).

Needless to say, a good supply of clean, fresh drinking water should always be available (*right*). Should your dog start regularly to drink more than normal amounts of water, contact your vet as this might indicate an internal disorder or onset of illness.

Below: *Commercial dog foods are available in different formulations that suit dogs of varying ages and conditions.*
A good diet will be reflected in the coat.

Allergies

These days lots of humans and pets alike suffer from allergies. Allergies are hypersensitive bodily reactions to allergens which can enter the body in one of three ways: inhalation, ingestion and absorption via the skin. Some may be minor in their effects, but others can be severely debilitating and troublesome. Finding out the cause of an allergy can take quite a time. A lot of allergies cause skin reactions which will be referred to as dermatitis, and often a trip to the vet can result in a prescription for steroids which mask the problem rather than sort it out.

In this section I would like to give you some ideas which may help towards solving the problem should your pet be unfortunate enough to suffer from one or more allergies.

PARASITIC ALLERGIES

• One of the easiest categories to identify and solve is allergies caused by external parasites. Often the pet is allergic to the saliva of fleas or lice. Their bites, together with the parasites' movement, will cause intense irritation: the animal will scratch and scratch and nibble at specific areas to relieve it. If not controlled, this scratching can cause open wounds and areas of distressed skin. Flea, tick and louse treatments, which can be in shampoo, spray or spot-on formulations, will easily solve this problem. Remember also to spray the home and bedding, too. Always carefully and fully read instructions on using these products as you will only derive the maximum benefit when they are used correctly.

CONTACT ALLERGIES

• Another category of allergy is the contact allergy. This is, as its name suggests, an allergic reaction to something with which the dog comes into direct contact, be it a natural material or manufactured product. The area that comes into contact with the offending substance will become red, raw and inflamed, and this can lead to constant scratching. By way of example, some dogs can be allergic to walking on grass, especially if it has been freshly cut. This can result in the dog's feet and toes becoming irritated. Other animals may be allergic to carpeting made from synthetic fibres, and will be affected on their tummies and the underside of their legs – the areas that come into contact with the carpet when they lie down. This type of allergy can also be caused by cleaning products used on carpets, especially the type which is shaken on in powder form and then vacuumed off. A lot of pets can be irritated by this. If your pet's irritation is only on its legs and undercarriage, the chances are that this is the result of a contact allergy.

Another group of products which can cause contact allergies are washing powders which may be used to clean the dog's bedding or perhaps the detergents used to wash towels used to dry a dog coming back wet from a walk. Again, this causes irritation, redness and possibly lack of hair growth. Changing to a different cleaning product should help.

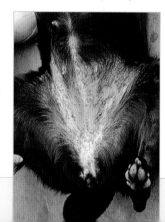

Left: *A typical allergic reaction causing irritation of the skin.*

Parasitic Allergies
Most commonly caused by flea bites, lice or mites.

Inhalant Allergies
Caused by natural substances, such as pollen and moulds, as well synthetic airborne chemicals, like air fresheners.

Food Allergies
Signs are usually an itchy skin or upset stomach.

Contact Allergies
The least common type, but nevertheless a problem for some dogs.

FOOD ALLERGIES

• The causes of other allergies which affect the whole body can be manifold, but one of the biggest is probably food. Many of today's complete meals used to feed pets contain a large collection of varied ingredients and additives. As with people, some dogs now have developed intolerances to substances like lactose, gluten, wheat etc., which may be found in prepared pet food products. Food allergies may result in patches of redness on the skin and constant scratching. If you think that your dog has a food allergy, try changing to another product or make up your own natural diet. Dogs may also scratch if they are being given too much red meat in their diet. If you want to try to analyse your dog's reactions to specific foods, remember it takes between four to six weeks before a new diet will have worked its way through the body. So don't look for instant results – you need to be patient.

INHALANT ALLERGIES

• Dogs can also be upset by air fresheners and fragrances used in room diffusers, so use them with caution. Some dogs also suffer from hay fever – another example showing that in many ways dogs can be as allergic to allergens present in their environment as we can. Discovering the cause of an allergy can often be time consuming and taxing, but do persevere for your dog's sake.

Dealing With Parasites

Parasites are all detrimental to a dog's state of health. They fall into two basic categories:
1) External (which means they are found on the outside of the body, on the skin), and
2) Internal (which means they are contained in the body).

EXTERNAL PARASITES

(Ectoparasites)
Regardless of how careful you are in keeping your dog clean and well-looked-after, it is very easy for a dog to pick up opportunistic parasites, that are always looking to hop on to a host dog for a quick meal. They can drastically affect the condition of a dog's skin and coat and may be encountered in any area of grassland or garden or even on the streets. Wild animals, including hedgehogs and foxes, are common spreaders of fleas and lice, as well as various forms of mange, which is a serious skin disease caused by mites – tiny parasites no larger than a pinhead (see page 20). Cats, too, will often bring home fleas after their hunting adventures, and these are easily passed on to dogs and are the host for tapeworm larvae (see page 22). Some ectoparasites are so small they cannot be seen with the naked eye, but the large majority can.

Basically, most external parasites cause the dog discomfort and irritation, which generally results in the dog shaking its head, persistently scratching and nibbling various parts of the body. The commonest ectoparasites are listed below.

Fleas
Description: Quite easily seen by the naked eye. They are small, slightly oval, dark brown, long-

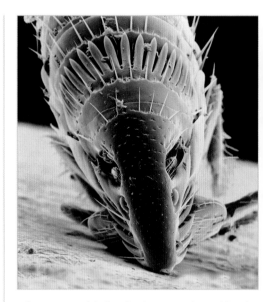

Above: *A adult flea feeding on a host's blood.*

legged, fast-leaping insects. It is said that the flea migrates around the dog's whole body every 24 hours. How can you tell if they are there? They leave small droppings which are very dark in colour and remain visible in the coat. Although dog fleas are different from cat and human fleas, they are not very discriminating and the insects will bite and feed on you, too. The flea actively bites the dog and sucks small amounts of blood from the animal. Some dogs are allergic to the saliva left in the bite wound and scratch intensely. The flea is also the host animal to the tapeworm, so if, while an animal is nibbling away at an itch, it ingests a flea, a tapeworm infestation of the gut might result, which can be very debilitating for the dog. Dogs that spend a lot of time outside can continually become re-infested with fleas.

Action and treatment: Fortunately, there are many ways that fleas can be got rid of. The best approach is initially to bathe your dog to get rid of the fleas and then use a proprietary treatment, which may be in the form of a spray, a treated collar or spot-on lotions. Do read the detailed instructions first as spot-on treatments must be used at least four days after a bath. Also remember to treat your house with a long-acting environmental spray. In very severe cases, a pest control service may be necessary. Vacuuming also helps to rid your house of fleas and their eggs which can remain dormant for up to two years in your carpets and furniture, waiting for an opportune moment to hatch, attach themselves to a host and start the whole cycle going again.

Ticks

Description: Usually picked up on land where sheep or deer have recently been grazing, mainly in spring and summer. They attach themselves by burying their mouth parts in the dog's skin, where they become engorged on the dog's blood and swell to the size of a small pea. When full of blood, they fall off. If a female tick has mated, she will lay her eggs in a mass and then die. The larvae that hatch from the eggs migrate up onto grass and vegetation and wait for another host animal to pass by to which they can attach themselves. This whole process takes from a few days to a week. Ticks are normally found around the head area and often on the ears, as the dog will push its head into undergrowth and the ticks very quickly latch on to it. Ticks should not be handled as some are carriers of Lyme disease, a bacterial infection which can be transmitted to humans and which can develop into a very

debilitating and serious illness.

Action and treatment: Some of the spot-on cures for fleas also are effective on ticks. Inexpensive tick tweezers can be purchased which help you to remove the whole tick by clasping and "unscrewing" it – which usually takes about three full turns. The mouthpiece of the tick will then come cleanly out of the skin leaving little trace of where it had been. (If you just use tweezers to pull the tick off, you will normally break it and leave the head of the tick under the skin, which can lead to local infection.) Or you can try putting some oil, such as olive oil, or Vaseline on and around the head section of the tick which hopefully will cause the tick to struggle for air and lose its grip.

Above: *The sheep tick,* Ixodes ricinus, *can also attach itself to dogs and gorge on their blood.*

Dealing With Parasites

Lice

Description: Lice are small, fat, wingless insects that inhabit a host animal's skin. There are two types of lice. Biting lice chew on your dog's skin, while sucking lice penetrate the skin and feed on tissue fluids. Lice lay tiny cluster of eggs called "nits" that can be seen sticking to the shafts of the deep hair. They are intensely irritating and should be treated promptly.

Action and treatment: Appropriate veterinary shampoos and some spot-on insecticide treatments are normally effective. You may also need to use a fine-toothed comb to rid the coat of nits.

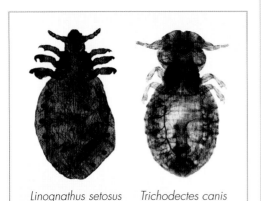

Linognathus setosus   Trichodectes canis

Mites

Description: Mites are tiny arthropods, some of which are parasitic on other animals. There are four main mites that affect dogs: two are mange mites (sarcoptic and demodectic) and two others (the fur mite, *Cheyletiella*, and harvest mites).

Let's deal with sarcoptic mange first. These microscopic mites burrow into the skin, often around ears and eyes of the dog, causing intense irritation, crusty scabs, lots of scratching, subsequent hair loss and body sores. Also a strong odour is detectable. Sarcoptic mange is highly contagious to other dogs and can cause scabies in humans.

Demodetic mange mites infect the hair follicles. Itching is much less acute, but nasty pustules often develop as a result of secondary infection. This type of mange is often hereditary.

Action and treatment for sarcoptic and demodectic mange: Sometimes a skin scrape needs to be taken and looked at under a microscope by a vet to confirm the diagnosis. Then standard veterinary shampoos should be used on a regular basis until the infection is cleared. Thorough cleaning or destruction of the pet's bedding is recommended as these mites can live for a short time off the dog's body.

Cheyletiella mites are just visible to the naked eye and form what looks like dandruff which, as they are often moving, has led to the colourful

Below: *A micrograph of the* Cheyletiella *mite.*

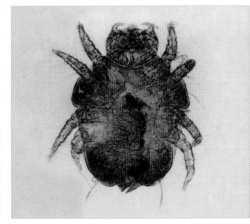

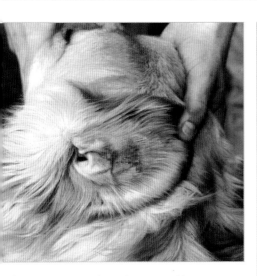

Above: *Crusty red patches caused by ear mites.*

description "walking dandruff". These mites cause a lot of skin scaling but with some irritation.

Action and treatment for *Cheyletiella* mites: These mites have a long life cycle so although a regular veterinary shampoo will easily clear them up, application does need to be repeated regularly for a few weeks. These mites are contagious through contact with other dogs. Bedding should be thoroughly cleaned, too.

The harvest mite is a very small, barely visible red mite. Its larvae usually infest field mice, and are frequently to be found in the summer and autumn around farmland and fields. They tend to attack only the feet and toes of dogs, causing them to lick and nibble around that area to relieve the irritation.

Action and treatment for harvest mites: Again, veterinary shampoos will easily take care of this condition.

Ear mites

Description: Strangely enough, while nearly all of the other mites are dark in colour, these little fellows are white and can just be seen by the naked eye, slowly walking around in the dark ear wax. They often cause the dog to shake its head and scratch its ears. They can easily be caught from cats.

Action and treatment: Gently clean surplus wax from around the ear flap, not probing into the ear. You can use an ear wipe or an alcohol-based ear cleaning product to do this. Once this is done, corrective ear drops or ear powder can be used following the directions on the packet. These products can easily be obtained from pet stores. However, if you are unsure of how to use them correctly or if your home treatment does not appear to solve the problem, seek veterinary advice.

Ringworm

Description: This is actually not a worm but a fungus that grows on the skin. It is highly contagious and can infect humans, so take care when handling a dog with ringworm. It first shows itself as a small, bald area (maybe half a fingernail in width), usually circular in shape, which looks irritated and slightly scaly. These patches may be found anywhere on the skin around the body. Often only one or two areas are affected, then it spreads as the infection progresses. They do not seem to cause a lot of irritation in dogs.

Action and treatment: Often a skin scrape taken by a vet will be necessary to identify this fungus. Once identified, veterinary creams and shampoos plus anti-fungal tablets will eradicate this condition. It is also sensible to vacuum your carpets and furnishings and to keep the dog's bedding clean to inhibit dispersal of fungal spores around the house.

Dealing With Parasites

INTERNAL PARASITES

(Endoparasites)

Internal parasites, normally various types of worms, are often transmitted by fleas, ticks, mosquitoes or snails and slugs. They can seriously impair a dog's health and some can cause contagious infectious diseases in humans (see Zoonoses on opposite page). Most dogs will have worms at some stage in their lives. The two most common kinds are roundworm, that are often inherited from the dog's mother, and tapeworm. Both of these are potential health hazards for humans. They are passed on to humans by finding their way into our blood streams and digestive systems via contact with dog faeces in which roundworm eggs are present. They can cause very serious health issues. This is another powerful argument in favour of picking up, in suitable poo bags, any faeces after your dog's bowel movements and disposing of the bag hygienically. You must also ensure that your dog is routinely wormed around every six months.

Roundworm

Description: The symptoms of roundworm are a pot belly, vomiting (sometimes bringing up worms which are threadlike and white in appearance), diarrhoea and sometimes passing worms in the faeces. The worms generally live in the dog's small intestine and take nourishment from the dog.

Action and treatment: Worm your dog regularly twice a year with a preparation approved by a vet. Some preparations cover both roundworm and tapeworm. If you suspect that your dog has worms, take a stool sample for your vet for laboratory analysis.

Tapeworm

Description: Tapeworms enter your dog's digestive system through larval ingestion via fleas. As the worms mature, they feed from matter in the dog's intestine causing it to feel hungry and so want to eat more. The worm attaches its head to the small intestine where it grows into a long chain of segments. These segments, which look like grains of rice, break off and can be seen in the dog's stools, beneath its tail and around the hair of the anus.

Action and treatment: Treatment must involve getting rid of the host fleas otherwise your dog is likely to be re-infected. Otherwise, treat as for roundworm.

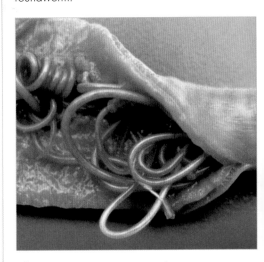

Above: Toxocara canis *roundworms seen in the dissected small intestine of an affected dog.*

Lungworm

When ingested by dogs, lungworm larvae, which are carried by slugs and snails as intermediate

TIP *For routine control of roundworms and tapeworms in adult dogs, regular anti-worming treatments conducted at six-monthly intervals are recommended. Puppies need a special worming course. Seek advice from your vet.*

hosts, can infect the bloodstream. The larvae migrate towards the heart and pulmonary arteries and thread-like adults develop which infest the pulmonary circulation. They cause coughing and breathing problems. As the dog coughs, it expels lungworm eggs which are also passed in faeces.

The eggs are ingested by slugs and snails and so the process starts again. In some cases the condition can prove fatal. Lungworm cannot infect humans.
Action and treatment: An effective worming product (some cover roundworm and tapeworm too) used regularly will prevent infestation.

ZOONOSES

By definition, zoonoses are infections or parasitic diseases that can be transmitted from animals to humans. They may include conditions caused by bacteria, viruses, fungi and parasites. It is important to know about them because of their health implications to you as a dog owner and members of your family.

Rabies

This is the single biggest danger in that infection, if untreated, is almost invariably fatal for both dogs and humans. The usual route for infection with the rabies virus is via a bite from an infected animal. Fortunately, thanks to long-standing laws on quarantine and the current health protection measures governing the movement of pets between countries, rabies infections are extremely rare in the United Kingdom, and are usually only acquired if an animal travels abroad. Many mammals other than dogs, such as monkeys and bats, can carry the virus. If you or your dog are bitten in a foreign country, you should seek professional medical help immediately.

Lyme disease

This is a very debilitating and serious condition. It can be caught by being bitten by infected ticks which spread the bacteria

causing the disease. Great care should be taken in dealing with any ticks which you may find on your dog and you should certainly not handle them with unprotected hands. For more information, see the advice given about Ticks on page 19.

Ringworm

This is a fungal infection of the skin which can easily be transferred from pets to humans. It is visible as a reddish or brown circle surrounding a patch of bumpy or roughened skin. It is relatively easy to treat with an antifungal cream from your doctor.

Worms

The possibility of contracting digestive parasites and other related illnesses through contact with dog excrement is small, but basic precautions should be taken to avoid contact between dog faeces and your hands. And of course all dog faeces in public places should be bagged up and removed by responsible owners. See also the section on Internal Parasites opposite.

Fleas

Dog or cat fleas might hop on to bite you but they do not live on humans. For the treatment of fleas, see the section on them on pages 18-19.

A handful of roundworms.

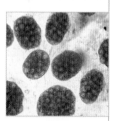

A tapeworm egg cluster.

A common dog flea.

Neutering and Changes ir

Nowadays many people, following veterinary advice, choose to neuter their female dogs as a matter of course, largely because they do not want the inconvenience and worry of dealing with a bitch that comes regularly into season. Also many vets recommend that it has long-term health benefits. For instance, it helps to eliminate the likelihood of mammary tumours later in life – though it does often make the dog more prone to put on weight if not carefully monitored. Similarly, with males, nearly all rescue societies and most animal welfare groups recommend neutering as the norm, saying that it will stop adult males straying in pursuit of bitches and prevent unplanned mating and unwanted litters.

When a dog is neutered, the organs that produce the hormones which control the dog's sexuality are removed. As a result the natural body cycle of coat change, which is linked to the reproductive cycle, is halted. A bitch will normally drop her coat (moult) after a season, and especially if she has had puppies. After neutering, the coat does not get the release signal – a hormone change – and thus the coat remains in place. This means the propensity to moult in bitches sometimes disappears and the growth of the undercoat often becomes very prolific, which in many breeds changes their looks quite dramatically.

The results of spaying and castration on pets with regards to their grooming can be quite great and differs quite

Yorkshire Terrier

significantly from breed to breed. I will try to sum up the effect neutering has on dogs of different coat types.

With very short- or single-coated breeds, e.g. smooth Dachshunds, Whippets, Dobermans, Weimaraners, Dalmatians, Pugs etc., there is no noticeable change to the coat pattern. With a lot of the double-coated breeds, such as Huskies, Samoyeds, Akitas, various spitz breeds, German Shepherds, corgis etc., there may be some more undercoat to groom but generally there is little change. The silk coats like the poodle and bichon are usually unaffected too.

Changes In Coat

But where it does make quite a lot of difference is in the combination coats, i.e. breeds which have both long and short hair, such as spaniels, setters and some of the retrievers. In these cases the coat on most of the body tends to become much softer and fluffier, and whereas before they would often have had a silky type of body coat and feathering on the back of the legs, it now becomes woolly and fluffier all over.

Breeds such as Lhasa Apsos, Shih Tzus, Afghan Hounds and Tibetan Terriers will grow a much

Left: *Bearded Collie coats are not noticeably altered by neutering.*

he Coat

Below: *The Cocker Spaniel naturally has a thick, silky coat which requires regular grooming to keep it looking good. If they are neutered, moulting is inhibited and the undercoat can grow very profuse.*

Ears and leg feathers need special attention.

thicker and denser coat, which owners will often decide to get clipped too. Lastly, the other breeds that can be affected are wire coated dogs. In their case the dog will often develop a softer coat and the wiry texture will disappear. Again this will usually have to be clipped rather than stripped, as is normally the case with wire coated breeds. In the case of these latter three groups, had the dog been clipped from the beginning the effect would be the same – a softer type coat, the harshness disappearing due to the constant clipping.

Left: *This spaniel has been neutered and it is immediately apparent that her coat has grown quite wild and woolly as a result. She has also put on weight – another undesirable side-effect.*

Effects of Age and Climate

STAGES OF THE COAT FROM PUPPYHOOD TO ADULT

The vast majority of puppies have quite different coats from the adult dog. Puppies have no secondary hairs – the coat consists of only primary hairs. The purpose of a puppy coat is to keep the youngster warm, so its fur appears quite downy and soft and grows out from the skin at almost a 90 degree angle. As the dog matures, the angle of growth of the hair decreases, reaching about 45 degrees in the adult.

From about the stage of 12 weeks of age secondary hairs will begin to emerge in the puppy's coat. By now the puppy should already be used to a regular grooming session and health check

(i.e. nails, teeth and ears). Other than in breeds with continuously growing coats, from this age onwards the puppy hair will start to be lost and replaced with a more mature type of coat. And this in its turn will be replaced at around 10-12 months with the adult coat.

In breeds with continuously growing coats, the quality of the hair shaft changes and becomes more mature as the puppy grows, with the puppy hair being retained at the end of the hair shaft. In some dogs, this will break off because it is a fragile type of hair, while in others, due to its softness, it will tangle with adjacent hairs forming mats if not carefully maintained. As before, this juvenile coat will be replaced at around 12-18 months with a fully mature coat texture. It is during these times when the coat is changing that you must be extremely efficient in your grooming to avoid severe matting.

The difference between the adult and the juvenile coats is very obvious in this picture.

THE EFFECTS OF THE WEATHER ON THE COAT

The natural cycle of nature take us through the four seasons of spring, summer, autumn and winter. And in the wild, animals' body clocks are governed by these changes and the length of daylight hours. In theory, autumn is the time to dispense with the summer coat and time to grow a new, fuller coat to help them to survive the winter; spring is the time to get rid of the thick undercoat ready for the warmth of summer. But few dogs who live in a domestic environment (i.e. your home) need to cope with cold weather. Instead they have to cope with central heating which tells the dog spring is here early – let's get rid of this heavy coat! – and this is when moulting and matting can occur if effective grooming (whether professional or home maintenance) is not carried out. The way this happens is that in winter the hair follicle closes and tends to hold on to the hair, whereas in the summer the follicle is more open and the hairs come away more often, making the coat thinner.

In summer when the sun is very hot, many people think that the coat is too much for their pet and that they are too hot. To some extent this may be true, but dogs do not sweat through the skin to cool down as we do. The way they have of cooling is through heavy panting: hot blood is brought to the enlarged tongue to be cooled by the air current. They may also sweat from the pads, and often seek cool places in which to lie down, like cold tiles or marble floors, to help maintain a lower overall body temperature.

In long coated or trimmed breeds, taking the hair very short in the summer months is not always the answer to stopping them feeling hot. Should the hair be taken very short the dog is more likely to suffer from sunburn to the skin. To make a human comparison, if you wear a T-shirt on the beach you may well feel cooler than without one. Overweight dogs feel the heat very easily.

With the very short coated breeds a sunscreen is frequently necessary to stop the dog from burning in the hottest sun, especially on the head and ears as these areas seem to burn easily. With some of the heavy coated breeds, if their coat is well cared for, air trapped between the layers will act as an insulator for the pet. One example is the Hungarian Puli which guards sheep flocks on the mountain slopes in its native country, where it can be very warm during the daylight hours but extremely cold at night. The air trapped between its coats acts as an insulator keeping the dog cool in the day and warm at night.

Then in autumn and winter we have a very damp, wet atmosphere which can cause a lot of matting and tangling in the coat if you do not keep on top of your pet's maintenance grooming. Mud, if left on long coated breeds, can rot the hair and is often very smelly. The best course of action here is, on returning from a walk, to put the dog's foot into a bucket or bowl (depending on the size of the dog) of tepid water and gently massage the hair. Slowly the mud will disintegrate and fall to the bottom of the bucket. Take the foot out and pat dry with a towel.

Matting and Moulting

MATTING – WHAT IS IT?

When looked at under a microscope, a single hair shaft looks very much like a rose stem with little barbs (cuticles) projecting along its length. Some hairs have many barbs along the shaft and others relatively fewer.

A typical mat of hair consists of a jumble of many coarse guard hairs criss-crossing one another. The guard hairs often end up catching and holding on to loose hairs from the finer undercoat. Once a tangle starts to occur in the guard hairs, the undercoat quickly clumps up very tightly. Dirt, dampness and friction will also cause mats to form.

You may find yourself in a situation where you have tried unsuccessfully to brush away or detangle a mat but still have most of it in place. It is possible with care to split the offending area into smaller sections with a mat breaker or small pair of scissors and these smaller clumps can then be brushed out individually.

If using scissors, hold the skin firmly at the root of the mat and, working away from the body, split the mat lengthwise into small strands

Below: *You can use a mat breaker to break down a serious tangle of hair bit by bit.*

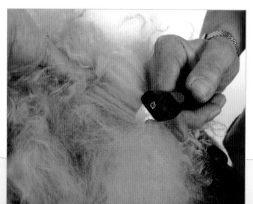

for further brushing out. Likewise, if using a mat breaker, hold the base of the mat without pulling on the dog's skin, and use as directed on the product's packaging.

If dealt with early using appropriate products and equipment, these mats can be broken down and removed. The use of an anti-static spray or, if bathing, a quality conditioner will tend to fill in the gap between the cuticle (barb) and the cortex (main hair shaft), thus reducing for a time the ability of the hairs to catch each other and tangle. (You should only attempt to bathe a dog if any tangles and mats in the coat are small.)

MOULTING AND HOW TO DEAL WITH IT

No matter what type of coat a dog has, some hair is shed and new hair grows in its place. Outdoor dogs shed their coat twice a year in autumn and spring, corresponding to the changes in the natural levels of daylight and temperature. Indoor dogs are not as exposed to changes in light levels, so they tend to shed their hair throughout the year – and as most owners have central heating too, the dog feels the warmth even in winter and attempts to get rid of its "winter" coat by moulting.

In some breeds you may not notice the process of moulting as it is so slight. This is obviously the case with the hairless breeds, and also with breeds which have continuously growing coats, such as the poodle, bichon and Bedlington Terrier. Unfortunately the greatest offenders when it comes to moulting and the breeds in which it is most difficult to control are

Left: *Dogs may roll to get rid of loose hair. A grooming mitt does the same job.*

before: the shed hair does not detach itself from the body coat unless it is groomed out. If this is not done, it leads to thick clumping and the formation of mats and tangles.

In the wild, at moulting times animals may be seen rolling in rough pasture land or rubbing their bodies against trees and bushes. To some extent this will help remove dead hair from the outer surface of the coat – and some of the

short haired dogs, such as the Pug, Jack Russell, Labrador, Beagle, Weimaraner and Staffordshire Bull Terrier. With these dogs, once the hair is loose it tends to just fall out, whereas with hairier breeds the loose hair tends to get trapped within the outer coat and form mats and tangles.

It helps if the dog is in a good, fit condition as the taut skin over a well muscled body holds on to the hair better than the slack skin of an overweight dog which tends to shed more hair.

Although in one respect short coats do not require regular grooming because they tend not to tangle, if anything they need just as much attention as longer-haired breeds because they seem constantly to be shedding hair which has the knack of lodging in household soft furnishings and getting all over your clothes. The most effective way of removing loose hair from clothes and furniture is either with a damp hand or with sticky packaging tape rolled around your closed hand with the sticky side outwards. Certain brands of vacuum cleaner claim to do a very good job of getting rid of animal hair around the house and one may be a worthwhile investment.

With medium to longer coats and double coats, moulting follows the same pattern as

behaviour will probably be for sheer enjoyment too! It is at moulting time that you should be diligent and thorough in your grooming. The correct use of a slicker type brush will help you remove most of the unwanted, dead, moulted hair as the little hook-type brush pins will grab the loose hair and help to pull it out. A pin brush, by contrast, will glide effectively through the hair but without removing the dead portions of the coat.

In the much longer coated breeds, such as the Afghan, Bearded Collies and Maltese, you may not be so aware of the moulting of dead hair as the long hair will come out in the course of general grooming. However, the moulting short undercoat will often come away from the skin a little distance but, because it does not reach the outer end of the hair shaft, patches of felting will occur near to the skin. Efficient and effective grooming will deal with this.

Unneutered bitches will often drop their coat in a big moult soon after a season or after having a litter of puppies. Sometimes the moult can be quite severe, but often a new coat is quickly formed. Unneutered dogs will generally hold on to their coats for much longer periods of time and moulting will be less noticeable.

Good Health & Hygiene

FOOT CARE

The feet play a very important role in safeguarding a dog's mobility and care should be taken to make sure they are healthy and clean. They should be checked regularly for dirt and tangled or matted hair, especially between the toe and pads, which may harbour foreign bodies (i.e. grass seeds and bits of grit or gravel). Such foreign bodies can sometimes turn into a small cyst between the toes if left in place. As a precautionary measure, it is a good idea during your grooming sessions to keep the hair between the toes trimmed, and likewise between the pads, so as to minimise the risk of the paws harbouring

specks of debris. It is a good idea to give your dog a foot bath in lukewarm water to help dislodge dirt etc. on a regular basis.

Check the bottoms of the pads, too. These can sometimes become dry and liable to crack and will benefit from the application of some pad wax or balm, which is available from your pet store.

In the winter, if salt has been put down on the road and pavements to help melt the snow, this has a very drying and cracking effect on dogs' pads. So do rinse paws on returning from a walk and perhaps apply some pad wax to keep the pads in good condition.

1

2

3

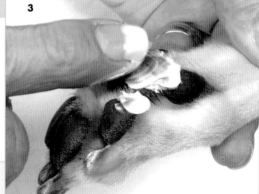

1: Carefully trim the hair growing around the pads and between the individual digits of the foot.
2: A warm foot bath will dislodge any mud or grit that has worked its way between the toes.
3: Pad wax or balm can be applied to pads that are cracking or showing signs of wear and tear.

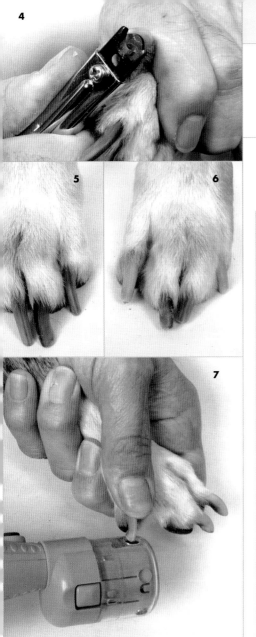

GUILLOTINE NAIL CLIPPERS

NAIL FILE

PLIER-TYPE NAIL CLIPPERS

NAIL CARE

Paying attention to the nails is a very important part of the grooming process for the comfort of the pet. Left unchecked, nails can grow to uncomfortable, painful and dangerous length, making them easily caught, damaged and even ripped out (very painful!). The whole of the dog's body is supported by the four feet, so we should make sure that the nails are a suitable length, not causing the toes to ache and disfigure and break down because the poor dog cannot put the pad down properly and squarely on the ground.

Not all dogs need the same amount of regular attention to the nails. It all depends on the shape of the foot and the amount of exercise the dog gets and whether it's on soft ground or hard. But the vast majority do, and it is really better and safer to take a little of the nail off on a regular basis rather than a lot all in one go. This is because, as the length of the nail grows, so does the quick running through it (see page 32).

Some dogs are totally indifferent to having their nails trimmed. Others dislike it with a passion. But you have to be in control, so, while at your grooming table, it can be useful to have someone to help you to hold your pet if necessary. Once you have taken hold of the foot, maintain control – if the pet jerks away, it learns bad habits, it "wins" – so gently continue. Keep the foot moderately low so as not to cause too much discomfort, getting your assistant to take a firm hold around the collar area if required, thus limiting flexion of the leg.

4: Nails should be clipped on a regular basis.
5 and 6: Overgrown nails (left) distort the lie of the foot. This is bad for the dog's stance and may cause damage. These nails after trimming (right).
7: This electric nail grinder has a guard on it to prevent you grinding away too much of the nail.

Good Health & Hygiene

HOW TO TRIM A NAIL

Trimming a white nail is fairly easy, for the pink of the quick (blood supply) can be seen easily. Place your nail clippers a little below where the pink stops and quickly make your cut. Black nails are a bit more challenging because the quick is not obvious. So start by taking off the hook at the end of the nail, look at the core of the nail and continue to cut off small sections until the flesh part starts to become white, which is as far as you should go without damaging the quick.

Safe Nail Clipping

Take several small clips, so you do not risk cutting the quick.

3rd
2nd
1st

QUICK

If cut, the quick will bleed quite profusely.

Once the correct length is established for one nail use it as a guide for the remaining nails. Should you accidentally trim the quick and end up with a bleeding nail, you can apply styptic powder (have a small pot on the shelf as a precaution) or hydrogen peroxide, or else apply corn starch or flour which will help stop the bleeding. Keep the pet quiet and still and the bleeding should stop quite quickly.

Nails can be trimmed with clippers or filed manually or electrically (see page 31). Do pay attention to the dew claw (the little nail just up from the pads). Dogs can have these on both their front feet and occasionally on their back feet, and as these don't reach the ground to be worn away, they can often grow right round and painfully back into the pad causing infection.

There are many different types of nail clippers and files, as you will see from the illustrations. Personally, I have found the guillotine type the easiest to use as it tends to slice the nail cleanly whereas pliers tend to squeeze, and sometimes crush, the nail. Filing is slow but quite efficient, and there is a new product on the market, an electric nail grinder with a safeguard on it, which is also most effective.

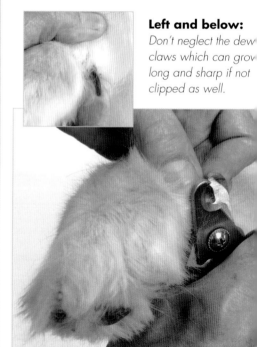

Left and below:
Don't neglect the dew claws which can grow long and sharp if not clipped as well.

EAR CARE

Dogs' ears are little wax makers. They come in various shapes and sizes – some upright, some long and pendulous, some small and some tipped over. Their care is slightly different depending on the type. Pendulous ears often need more care than the others: because of the overhanging fold wax will tend to remain in the ear canal, and the closeness of the ear flap against the dog's cheek means that the ear retains moisture which, combined with the warmth, makes for an ideal breeding ground for ear mites. Whatever the type, you should check them and make sure they are free from foreign objects and of surplus wax. This can be done by using an ear wipe specially formulated to clean the wax away. Do not probe too deeply into the ear. Again, do this while at your regular grooming session at your grooming station, maybe checking this weekly unless there is an evident problem which needs more immediate attention.

Some long haired breeds have hair that constantly grows in the ear canal. This can cause problems due to the lack of air getting to the ear canal, or by preventing the natural escape of wax. These breeds need to have the hair plucked from the ear canal. This should ideally be done by a vet or qualified groomer on a regular basis. It is also possible to do it yourself if you are careful and take some expert advice first, but it can make the ears sensitive if not done properly.

Should the ear start to smell or if a discharge is apparent, veterinary help should be sought.

33

Right: *Use a proprietary ear wipe to clean your dog's ears. You are aiming to remove wax and dirt from the external fold of the ear and the opening to the ear canal. Don't probe too deeply, or start using cotton buds – you may cause damage.*

Good Health & Hygiene

EYE CARE

On a daily basis, you should pay attention to your dog's eyes. Many breeds – including most of the long haired and the short nosed breeds – will get a collection of matter forming around the inner corners of their eyes. An eye wipe or moist piece of cotton wool wiped gently across the corner of the eye will normally remove this. Should the eye seem inflamed or have a discharge, seek veterinary advice.

Staining: Some light-coloured dogs suffer from tear staining leaving marks on the fur of the muzzle under the eyes. This is caused by the acidity of the tears. It may also occur in darker-coated dogs, but naturally this tends to be less noticeable. There are many products on the market that can help with this and gentle bathing with a suitable proprietary product, of which there are many in pet stores, helps keep it to a minimum.

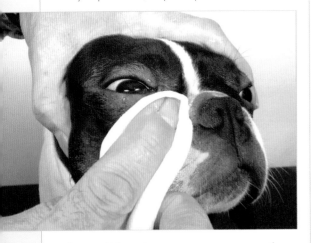

Above: *When cleaning eyes, wipe away from the eye itself along the line of the nose.*

TEETH AND THEIR CARE

Proper dental care is one of the most neglected aspects of pet care. You should regularly check your dog's teeth, making sure that there is no sign of gum infection or tartar build-up on the teeth, which can progress to bad breath, tenderness of the mouth (gum infection or gingivitis) and eventual loss of teeth.

Plaque is the same for a dog as it is for us – a bacteria-laden film forming on the teeth. This can then calcify on the teeth to form tartar. If not kept under control, the bacteria get into the gum tissue, causing inflammation, and then attack the roots of the teeth. The jaw bone in which the teeth are situated then begins to erode and eventually the rotten teeth fall out. You can help to reduce the incidence of plaque/tartar by giving your dog a complete dry dog food and/or hard biscuits, chew toys, rawhide or sterile bones to chew on, many of which can be found in good pet stores.

But the best way to control plaque and tartar is to brush the teeth. This may sound silly, but when the puppy is young and on the grooming table, start to massage its teeth and gums and get it used to feeling your fingers in its mouth. You can buy specially made brushes and toothpaste for dogs. Don't use toothpaste formulated for humans as most dogs will not like the taste, it foams too much and often makes them sick. I suggest brushing your dog's teeth at least a couple of times a week (daily is better if you have the time).

Professional descaling by a vet is sometimes needed if the condition of the teeth gets quite bad. If not attended to, bad teeth can have quite a detrimental effect on the pet's overall well-being.

TIP *If your dog resists your attempts to introduce a handled toothbrush into its mouth, consider using a finger brush – this is like a small flexible thimble that slips over the end of your forefinger.*

Unfortunately, a lot of smaller breeds seem to have weaker teeth and they often start to lose them at a relatively early age.

Below: *If your dog is unused to toothpaste, first put some on a finger and rub it on its gums.*

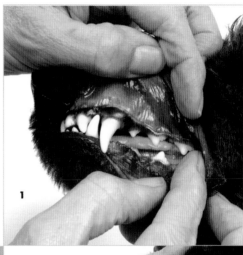

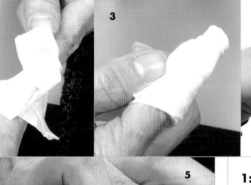

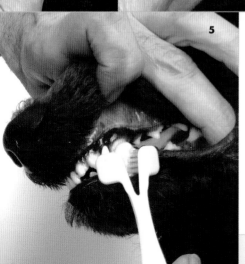

1: Make a dental check-up a regular part of your grooming routine – it will pay dividends.
2: Dental tooth wipes are impregnated with special chemicals that help to freshen breath and combat the build-up of plaque on the teeth.
3: Wrap a clean wipe around your index finger.
4: And then rub it gently around the teeth and gums in both upper and lower jaws.
5: For more systematic cleaning, use a dog toothbrush and properly formulated toothpaste. This double-headed brush is very effective.

Care Routine Guide

		DAILY	WEEKLY	MON
TEETH See page 34	BRUSHING TEETH			
	OWNER CHECK / DECAY			
	VET CHECK / DESCALING			
EYES See page 34	DISCHARGE / STAINING	DISCHARGE		STAIN
	TRIMMING BROWS			
EARS See page 33	WAX DEPOSITS			
	HAIR GROWTH IN EARS			
FEET See page 30	NAILS AND DEW CLAWS			
	PADS / HAIR TRIM		PADS	
BATHING / DRYING See pages 46-75	SMOOTH / SHORT COATS			
	WOOL / WIRE COATS			WO
	LONG / HEAVY COATS			
GROOMING See pages 76-139	SMOOTH / SHORT COATS			
	WOOL / WIRE COATS			
	LONG / HEAVY COATS			
WORMING	ADULT DOGS			

TIP *Try to make these care recommendations part of your regular routine. Dogs thrive in a routine pattern and should quickly come to accept that frequent physical check-ups are nothing to worry about.*

ONTHLY	QUARTERLY	6 MONTHLY	YEARLY		
					• Ideally teeth should be brushed daily, but if this is not possible, try to do it at least once a week. • Descaling teeth is a job best left to a vet.
					• Products are available which you add to the daily feed to combat staining around the eyes.
					• Dogs with pendulous, overhanging ears will need more frequent aural check-ups.
	HAIR TRIM				• Front nails grow more quickly than back claws. • Checks pads more frequently in winter.
	WIRE				• Of course, intervals between baths depend very much on your personal circumstances. An outdoors-loving dog will naturally get dirtier than a couch potato!
					• The rule of thumb is that the longer the hair, the more often you should groom the dog. • Also as a puppy grows into an adult dog, you should groom more often.
					• An adult dog should be wormed twice a year.

Grooming Equipment

BRUSHES

Brushes come in various shapes and sizes, and they have been designed for specific purposes. People tend to buy brushes that are too soft for the purpose for which they are required. There are four main types.

Slicker: One of the best grooming brushes to buy is the slicker style. Although it may look a little fierce, it is a very useful, efficient and practical brush to have in your grooming kit. It is considered an all-purpose brush and can be used on all but the short, fine coated breeds, such as the Whippet or Boxer. It is important to use it correctly as it can injure your pet by scraping the skin and causing brush burn if used incorrectly.

For correct use, hold the brush lightly at the base of the handle where it joins the head of the brush containing the wire pins. Practise some brush strokes first before using: you should be aiming for a sliding motion. Try testing it on your arm to get an idea of the correct amount of pressure you need to apply – you will be surprised at how light it is. Brush with the majority of the pad in contact with the dog. Once mastered, you will be surprised at how well you do. Even difficult tangles can be removed without causing discomfort to your dog. Take time to work systematically over the dog ensuring all parts are brushed thoroughly. Start at the lowest part of the body and work your way up – e.g. start at the toes and gently work up the leg. On longer coats, start brushing at the edges or ends of the hair and gently work towards the skin rather than immediately putting the brush at the base of the hair and pulling through the whole coat.

Slicker Brush An efficient brush for working on all coat types except fine, smooth hair.

1 Gauge the correct amount of pressure to apply by testing brush strokes on your arm

Slicker Brush An alternative lighter-weight design.

The pins all lean in one direction.

Pin brush: This is generally used on a well-groomed, long, flowing coat and employed in conjunction with a spray of anti-static coat conditioner. Used on a regular basis, this can be a very successful method of grooming. Brush with easy action strokes, helping the brush glide through the coat rather than stabbing at the hair. Again, start at the lowest point to the ground and work your way up the dog. Also, start brushing at the end of the hair shaft, with each successive stroke going further in towards the skin, thus untangling hairs from the end before moving towards the root. This brush will have little or no effect on badly knotted or tangled hair.

TIP *A rubber grooming glove is very useful for pulling loose hair from smooth and short coated breeds. The raised rubber knobbles drag out moulted hair, and also massage and invigorate the skin.* **Grooming Glove**

Pin Brush A gentler brush than a slicker – useful for long, flowing coats.

Bristle Brush A softer brush for using on short and smooth coats. Nylon bristles can cause a build-up of static.

1

2 The reddened area of skin shows that over-vigorous use of a slicker is likely to cause the dog some discomfort.

2

Rubber Brush Removes dead hair and massages the skin.

Short bristle brush: These brushes can come in many shapes and sizes, with handles or without, and with different bristle textures from hard to soft. This is a useful and effective brush for smooth and short coated breeds. The stiffer type of bristle is good for breeds such as Labradors as it can brush away dirt and loose hairs from this quite coarse type of coat. The softer brushes are more suited to coats such as those of Boxers or Whippets.

Rubber brushes: Also very good for smooth coated dogs are the rubber brushes which are available in various sizes and different tooth patterns. These little rubber fingers grip the short, loose hairs very effectively and pull them out of the body coat. You will be amazed how much loose hair you can remove with these. They also give the skin a good massage along the way. You don't really need to follow a pattern when using a rubber brush, as long as you work all over the whole body and legs of course. You can brush up and down or in a circular pattern, whichever you find most effective.

Another very efficient "home-made" grooming tool is a pair of domestic washing up gloves with the little knobbles on the fingers because they allow you to glide over the body easily.

Grooming Equipment

COMBS

The best type of comb for general grooming purposes is a double ended comb about 20cm (8-9in) long with two types of teeth: a fine section with close spacing and a coarse section where the teeth are set further apart. Before combing, you first brush your dog to remove any tangles and debris from the coat. This should be followed by combing with the coarser end which will remove and unclog the hair still more, and then finally you use the fine end of the comb to make sure no loose bits of moulting hair are left in the coat which might start the tangling process again. On longer coated breeds a little anti-static spray will make progress easier.

Pick a comb with reasonably pointed teeth so as to penetrate the hair when you are running it through the coat. If you buy one with very blunt teeth, it will not penetrate the coat so easily and your grooming will not be as effective.

COAT CLIPPERS

There are quite a lot of clippers on the market. Many of them say they are suitable for trimming a pet's coat and use a selection of plastic combs that fit over a set blade. As with many things in life, this is often a case of you get what you pay for. So do study the capabilities of the clipper.

Which clippers to buy also depends on how experienced you are at using them correctly and the condition of the dog you are to clip. If you intend to clip your dog on a regular basis, you would be wise to purchase a slightly more expensive pair of clippers that you can rely on to get a good job every time.

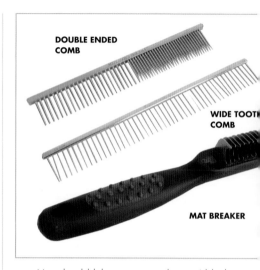

DOUBLE ENDED COMB

WIDE TOOTH COMB

MAT BREAKER

You should lubricate your clippers' blade with oil after use to help protect its edge and stop it from jamming. Store in a warm, dry place as dampness will cause rust and blunt the blade.

Do take care with clippers. They can upset some dogs and may lead to nicks and cuts in unpractised hands. If in any doubt, leave clipping to a professional groomer.

NAIL CLIPPERS AND FILES

There are many different styles of nail clippers. The easiest and most effective to use I find is the guillotine style as this slices through the nail making a clean cut. This style generally comes in two sizes – large and small. With the plier type you tend to squeeze the nail before the cutting action starts, and I find that it's not so easy to have precise control over them. See the section on nail care (pages 31-32) for advice on how to trim nails safely.

TIP *Try to keep one hand on the dog all the time that you are grooming it. It restricts its ability to move around, helps to reassure it that you are in control and also somehow keeps you calmer too.*

GUILLOTINE NAIL CLIPPERS

ELECTRIC CLIPPERS FOR HOME USE

TRIMMING SCISSORS

PLIER-TYPE NAIL CLIPPERS

PROFESSIONAL CLIPPERS

NAIL FILE

41

For many, the safest and perhaps easiest way to trim the nails is by gentle filing. This is best done on a regular basis, perhaps monthly, and will, if done correctly, keep the length of the nails under control. You can use either a regular dog nail file similar to an emery board, or there are now electric rotary nail grinders that are very effective (see page 31).

MAT BREAKERS

These are very effective when used correctly. They are made up of a row of about six hooked teeth on a body with a handle. The teeth on the front side have a recessed blade cutting edge. First, hold on to the skin and hair surrounding the mat with your left hand to avoid pulling on the dog's skin, then place the tips of the hooked teeth carefully at the root of the mat or knot. Apply pressure to the mat breaker and pull it through the knot or mat, thereby virtually cutting it into

small parts. If the knot or mat is large, you may have to do this a few times. After breaking the mat down into smaller tangles, revert to using your slicker brush to disperse them, brushing it down to the end of the hair shaft and clean away from the body. This can take quite some patience, both from you and your dog.

Damage can also be done with this implement if used incorrectly. It is possible to catch and tear the skin. That is why it is essential to place your other hand near the base of the mat and to make sure exactly where the cutting blades are going before you exert any pressure.

SCISSORS

Scissors come in various shapes and sizes. Choose longish blades with rounded ends that are safer when trimming around pads and sensitive areas like eyebrows and anus. Keep the blades clean, oiled and dry to maintain the edge.

Shampoos and Sprays

In recent years many advances have been made in the general availability and suitability of grooming products for dogs. Bear in mind, however, that what is suitable for one coat type is not necessarily suitable for a different coat type. They can be very diverse and quite technical products, many meant for show preparation. Here I shall describe some of the more popular preparations that you might find useful. In these days of environmental concern, you will find that many of these products are made to be biodegradable.

ANTI-STATIC GROOMING SPRAYS

For medium to longer hair breeds, an anti-static grooming spray makes regular grooming much easier. A light spray of the product helps to restore and maintain the natural moisture that should be in the hair. It also helps to remove tangles and control static and flyaway coats, repels dirt by very slightly coating the hair shafts and makes the hair more pliable and less likely to break.

SHAMPOOS

They come in such a vast range, but to start with you must remember that the pH of a dog's skin is different from a human's, and that it also differs from breed to breed. So it is not advisable to use human

shampoo products on any dog.

Within the dog range not all shampoos will be suitable for all dogs, so you must read and follow the advice on labels carefully, especially with regard to dilution rates. Your dog's lifestyle and the frequency with which you bathe him or her will influence your choice of a suitable product. If your dog is bathed very frequently, it will benefit from a gentler shampoo than one that is perhaps only bathed once a year!

This list that will give you an idea of the range of shampoos that are available:
- general deep cleansing
- flea and tick control
- for problem skin
- for dry and brittle coats
- conditioning
- colour enhancing
- hypoallergenic, for dogs with sensitive or allergic skin reactions
- tearless, for use near eyes

In addition, there is a range of veterinary prescribed shampoos for specific skin and coat problems. And there is also a product you can put on after bathing to help reduce the dander produced by dogs which can cause allergies in humans.

Left: *There are many different types of shampoo available for dogs. Check that your chosen product is suitable for your dog's coat.*

TIP *To get your dog really clean, it is advisable to shampoo its coat twice during a bath. The first lather strips out dirt and oils allowing the second application to penetrate more deeply.*

CONDITIONERS

As with shampoos, there is quite an extensive range of conditioning products available, with many formulations having special benefits depending on coat/skin type and the health of the dog's hair. Again, it is essential to read labels and observe recommended dilution rates.

Not all dogs need a conditioner. On many of the double and spitz-type coats, using conditioner would put you at a disadvantage when drying as it would encourage all the loose coat to remain in place, clogging up the condition of the general coat.

But for a lot of dogs, especially those with continuously growing, long haired coats (rather than the shorter or double coated types) conditioners are very useful and beneficial. They help to moisturise and nourish dry and damaged hair and skin by coating the hair shaft and skin and closing down the cuticles (the outermost layer of the hair consisting of a hard, shingle-like layer of overlapping cells) making the individual hairs more stable and pliable, and less likely to tangle.

The appropriate conditioner type is dependent on the coat type. The dilution rate is also relevant: heavy conditioners are good for dogs with a drop type coat as they help the coat to lie better, and the lighter conditioners are suitable for the more fluffy types of coat, allowing them to be nourished but still look full and voluminous.

By removing static, conditioners help maintain the quality of a dog's coat and, if used properly, they minimise maintenance grooming between baths.

FLEA ERADICATION AND PREVENTION

Although they may not strictly be grooming products, I should mention here those products aimed at flea eradication and prevention. Fleas are nowhere near as common as they were some years ago, but they are still unwelcome visitors that your dog does not need or want. Some animals don't seem to mind them too much, but to the vast majority of dogs they cause varying levels of distress. Some dogs are very allergic to the fleas' saliva and will scratch themselves raw after being bitten, and of course it is unsettling for an owner to see a dog looking so uncomfortable and causing itself upset.

Should you live in an area where pets easily pick up fleas, prevention is the best route to follow. This is easily done by using a spot-on capsule emptied at the meeting point of the shoulder blades (an area where the dog cannot lick), and this should give immunity for one month, or up to three months depending on the brand used. You can also use sprays on a dog or attach flea collars, but I find that the spot-on treatments seem to be the most effective.

Of course, should your pet end up with fleas, the dog will inevitably bring them into the house where they will colonise in the soft furnishings and carpets on which they will lay their eggs. And so the next generation is on its way. It is a sobering thought to realise that in its lifetime each adult female flea can lay between 400 and 500 eggs. Again, prevention is the best policy.

You can read in more detail about fleas in the parasite section (see pages 18-19).

43

PART TWO

Bathing

Drying

Grooming

Parlour Tips

• General advice concerning the do's and don't's of bathing your dog. This section provides information about the products that you will need, preparing your dog for the bath, shampooing, rinsing and applying conditioner. **46-51**

• More specific bathing advice relating to different coat types is provided here as well as detailed directions on how best to dry dogs with different coat types, and the safe use of an electric hand dryer where appropriate. **52-75**

• Eight coat types are described and typical breed examples listed. Illustrated step-by-step sequences show how each type of coat can best be groomed at home, along with essential care routines for eyes, ears, teeth and nails. **76-139**

• A professional shares with us his inside knowledge: how to groom older dogs, dealing with common problems, things **not** to do, how to assess if your dog is good enough to show, and times when professional help is called for. **140-143**

Bathing Your Dog

You will find more specific coverage about bathing dogs according to their coat type after this introductory section. However, before you get started, here are a few pointers which should help to make the process a little easier for all concerned, no matter what your dog's coat type.

First, collect all the things that you need before you start and place them within easy reach:

- **Cotton wool** for blocking ears.
- **Non-slip mat** for the bath.
- **Shampoo, conditioner** if needed.
- **Towels**.
- **Jug** or other container for mixing shampoo.
- **Lightweight collar** to help you keep control of your dog (fabric collars or chain are best – do not use leather as it can stain the hair when the collar gets wet).

Once all these items are in place and your shampoo is mixed (read the dilution instructions on your chosen product), take your dog to the bathing area and close the door! The last thing you need is a half-shampooed dog running amok about your house with you in hot pursuit.

Place your dog on the secure anti-slip mat in the bath. **Tip:** It's often easier if two people are available for the task of bathing a dog, one to hold the dog and one to wash, so try to get another household member to help. Put a plug of cotton wool gently in each of the dog's ears to prevent water getting into the ear canal.

Whether you are using a jug to pour water over your dog or a shower hand attachment, make sure before you start that the water temperature is suitable: just around warm. Don't use water that is hot. Thoroughly wet down the dog all over, but leave the head area dry for the time being. (Once their heads are wet, dogs may need to shake.) Then shampoo thoroughly using enough shampoo to work up a rich lather. Applying the shampoo, suitably diluted, with a wet sponge can be very effective. If you feel it's necessary because the dog is particularly dirty or the shampoo isn't lathering too well, partially rinse and apply a second shampoo. Rinse most of the shampoo from the coat.

Now turn your attention to the dog's head, washing it carefully with a tear-free shampoo. Then rinse the whole dog thoroughly until the coat is squeaky clean when you run your hands over it. (Remember that leaving shampoo in the coat can lead to skin irritation.) If you are going to use a conditioner, now is the time to do so, rinsing thoroughly as before.

If possible, let the dog shake before you start to towel him dry as this will get rid of a lot of surplus water. Try to hold on to your dog as he shakes, whether this is in the bath, on the floor or on your grooming table, so he doesn't choose this moment to scoot off! Then towel dry as much as possible. For more details on the best methods of drying, see the bathing and drying instructions according to coat type that follow this section.

If you don't want to do all this at home, some big pet stores have bathing facilities that you can hire for around 30 minutes, with a big tub and power dryer – meaning you don't make any mess at home.

1

2

3

: Assemble all the items that you will need.
so brush the dog thoroughly all over to get
d of any loose hair before you start.
: Gently block the entrance to each ear
anal with a small plug of cotton wool.
: Check that the water is just around warm –
ot hot – and place the dog in the bath.

continued overleaf ▶

BATHING YOUR DOG *continued*

4: Put a small quantity of shampoo into the bath water and use this mix to wet the coat. You do not want to put shampoo directly onto dry hair.

5: Now pour pre-diluted shampoo onto the coat and massage it in to work up a rich lather.

6: Once the body is well shampooed, you may also wet the ears in preparation for lathering them. But only work on the ears at this stage; the head comes later.

7: Work diluted shampoo into the ears. Be careful not to get lather near the dog's eyes.

8: Rinse off the lather and, if the dog is quite dirty, re-shampoo. Then partially rinse clean.

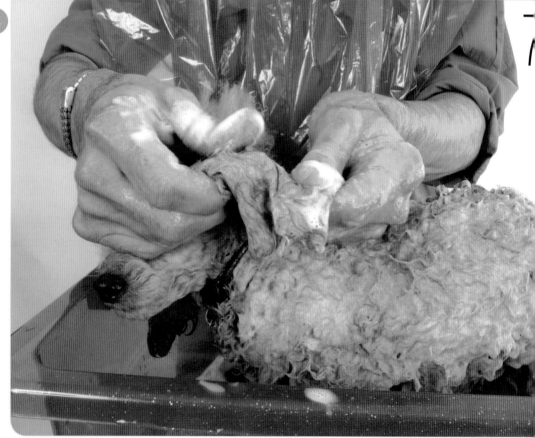

continued overleaf ▶

BATHING YOUR DOG *continued*

9: Now for the head: first wet the head with clean, warm water. Be careful near the eyes.

10: Apply a tear-free shampoo to the head observing any dilution recommendations.

11: Work the lather all around the head and muzzle but do try to avoid getting soap lather directly into the dog's eyes.

12: Rinse the dog thoroughly all over using jugs of clean, warm water or a shower attachment. You may need to rinse twice. Cover the eyes with your hand when rinsing the head.

13: Remove the ear plugs, let the dog shake and wrap in a towel in preparation for drying.

SMOOTH AND SHORT

BATHING AND DRYING

Preparation: First, make sure you have to hand all the equipment that you require before starting: towels, shampoo etc. All pre-bath work should be done at your grooming station. It is important to keep to a regular pattern, which will make you and your pet feel more secure about the process. Check the ears to see if they need cleaning. Use an ear wipe if necessary and then plug each ear with cotton wool to stop water getting in. (And do remember to remove the cotton wool after the bath!).

• Use a quality, regular, all-purpose shampoo, massaging lather into all parts (see Bathing Your Dog section on pages 46-51). Rinse and put on a light conditioner if needed and rinse again.

• Towel dry as much as possible. Allow the coat to dry naturally on a warm day, or use a hair dryer until the dog is completely dry. You can use a regular human hair dryer on a low or medium setting, depending on the dryer. Dry the main body first, not keeping the dryer in one place for too long, then move on to the legs. Dogs generally do not like dryers around the head, ears and eyes so great care must be shown here. And, of course, avoid getting the hair dryer wet. It is dangerous to operate any electrical device in the presence of water.

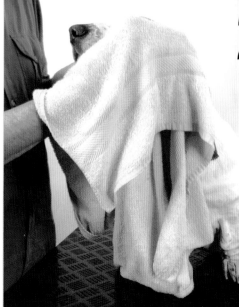

COATS

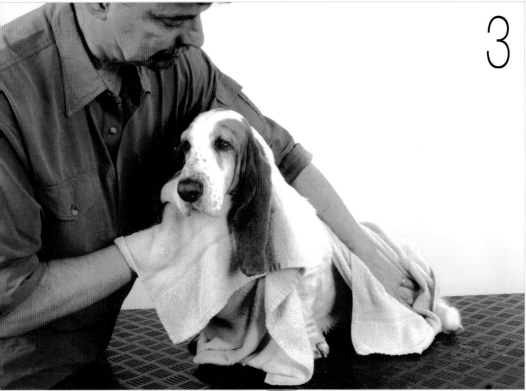

3

4

1: Start by towelling dry as much of the body and underside as possible. Dogs often want to shake themselves when their coats are wet, and you should let the dog do this if it is so inclined.

2: Then towel around the head, paying particular attention to the ears and jowls if they are pendulous like this Basset's.

3: Work round to the back end and towel up and down the legs.

4: If the dog has a stout tail, it is quite useful to grab this as a "handle" to give you extra control while drying the rump.

continued overleaf ▶

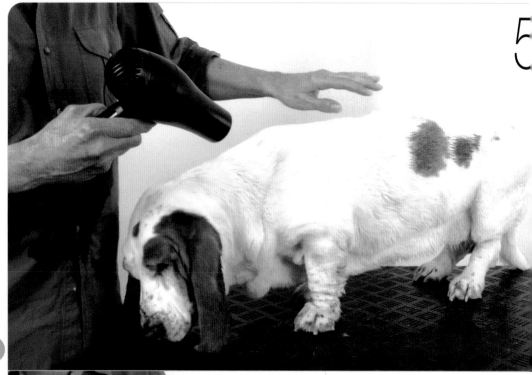

5

54

6

5: Then set to work with a hand dryer on a low or medium setting. Don't have the temperature set too hot – test it for comfort on your hand first.

6: Gently hold the ears out so that the air from the dryer can circulate. But be careful using a dryer around the head – some dogs will shy away from it.

7: Use either your hands or a bristle brush to tease up the lie of the hair so that the warm air can get down to the roots. It's no good just drying the top layer and leaving some of the coat wet

8: Work the brush under the airflow in all directions, both with and against the nap of the coat. A low-slung dog like this might prefer to lie down.

9: It should only take 10 minutes or so to complete the job – but be thorough.

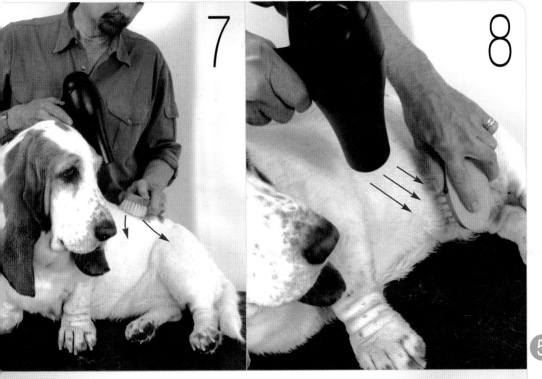

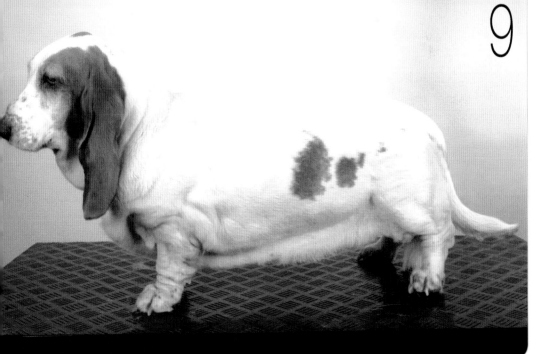

COMBINATION COAT

BATHING AND DRYING

Preparation: First, make sure you have to hand all the equipment that you require before starting: towels, shampoo etc. All pre-bath work should be done at your grooming station. It is important to keep to a regular pattern, which will make you and your pet feel more secure about the process. Check the ears to see if they need cleaning. Use an ear wipe if necessary and then plug each ear with cotton wool to stop water getting in. (And do remember to remove the cotton wool after the bath!)

• Thoroughly brush the coat through before placing the dog in the bath. Use a regular, quality, all-purpose shampoo unless another type of product is required. Get your fingers deeply into the coat, making sure that you massage everywhere down to the roots of the hair with the shampoo, especially under the front legs, around the back of the ears, breeches and groin area, and along the belly. Rinse thoroughly. Put suitable conditioner on the fringing on the back of the front legs, shirt front, tummy, rear of the hind legs and tail fringes. Leave on as long as instructed and then rinse thoroughly.

• Vigorously hand towel dry. Brush hair with the flow of the coat, making sure that the longer fringe hair is free of tangling. Then begin drying with the dryer, set to medium warm, fast speed, again brushing in the direction in which the coat grows to allow it to lie close to the skin. After drying is finished, groom through with a comb.

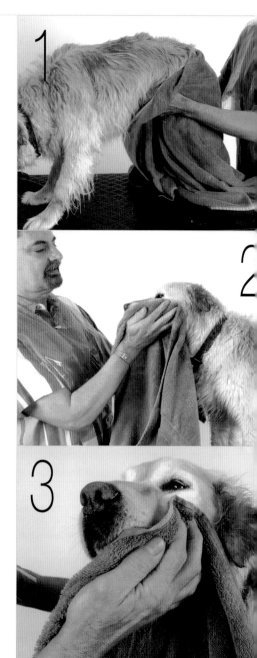

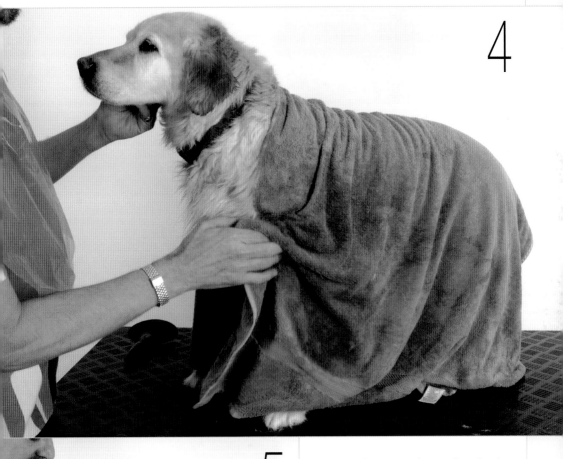

4

5

1: Begin by vigorously towelling the dog dry as it stands on the grooming table.
2: Try to dry the head quite early on as if the ears are left wet, the dog will have a natural tendency to shake.
3: Don't forget the face and muzzle.
4: As the coat starts to dry, wrapping the towel over the body also allows body heat to have a drying effect.
5: Towel paws and the leg featherings.

continued overleaf ▶

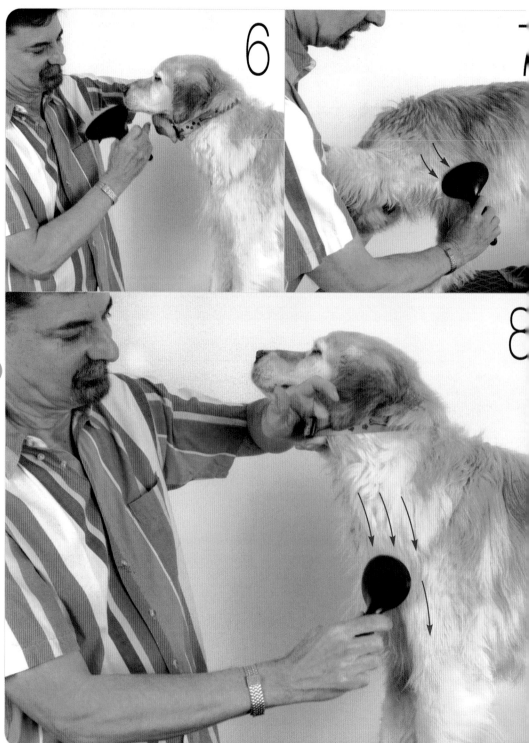

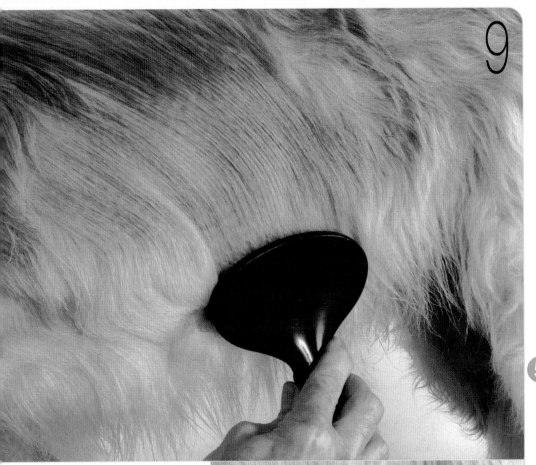

6: The next task is to brush all the coat to make sure that it is tangle-free and that any dead hair is brushed out. It helps if you hold the collar for control.

7: Stretch a leg forward to gain access to the friction areas underneath.

8: Continue to brush around the chest and the front quarters.

9: Make sure that the brush penetrates all the way through the coat rather than just gliding through the surface layer. Use fairly short, easy brush strokes.

10: You will find that the slicker brush removes a remarkable amount of hair.

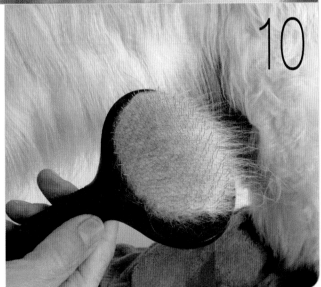

continued overleaf ▶

60

11

12

11: Now use a dryer along with the slicker brush.

12: Blow in the direction of hair growth to avoid fluffing up the coat and making it messy. Use an easy wrist action with the brush. Move the dryer around so that it is not directed too long on any one part of the dog.

13: This detail shows the undercoat. The dryer allows you to see where this hair is clumpy. You must brush out any tangling or "felting" here.

14: Five brush-loads of hair were removed from this dog after its bath and drying routine.

15: Finish off with a thorough comb through the coat and furnishings.

16: Clean, dry and looking good.

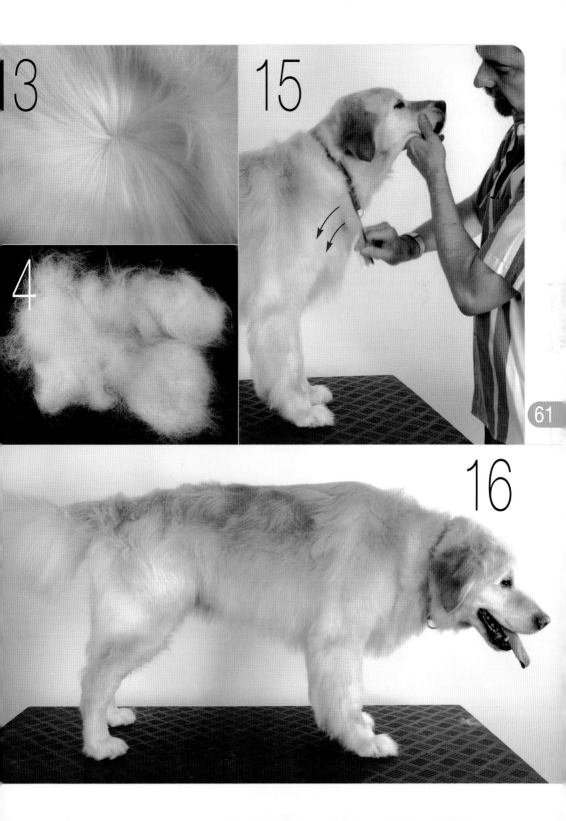

DOUBLE COATS

BATHING AND DRYING

Preparation: First, make sure you have to hand all the equipment that you require before starting: towels, shampoo etc. All pre-bath work should be done at your grooming station. It is important to keep to a regular pattern, which will make you and your pet feel more secure about the process. Check the ears to see if they need cleaning. Use an ear wipe if necessary and then plug each ear with cotton wool to stop water getting in. (And do remember to remove the cotton wool afterwards.)

• Make sure that you have given a thorough brush through this thick, dense type of coat, paying special attention to the areas around the ears, the backs of the front and hind legs, the tail, the tummy and the shirt front. Use a quality, all-purpose shampoo unless another type of product is required. Get your fingers deeply into the coat, making sure you massage the shampoo down to the roots of the hair everywhere, and especially the areas mentioned above where the hair is particularly dense. Rinse off. If the dog is very dirty, perhaps half rinse off and reapply shampoo to the very thick areas, thereby making sure you have really got the dog as clean as possible. Thoroughly rinse until squeaky clean. Apply conditioner generously to very thick areas of coat to help with drying, and less generously to the body coat. Rinse again.

• Towel dry vigorously and start drying with a hair dryer. You will get quite a lot of loose hair with this coat type. Dry in the direction of coat growth. Using a firm slicker brush will make sure you get down to the skin and it will help to remove stubborn dead coat and tangles and let you progress through the job efficiently. After drying is finished, groom through with a comb.

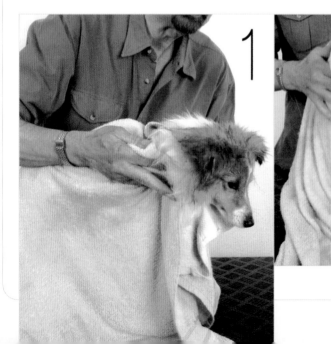

3

This type of coat will absorb quite a
of water so it will benefit from a brisk
welling before the dryer is used.

Start at the head and then work back
wn the body to the hind quarters and
l. Also towel dry the furnishings and
gs, chest and underside.

Now turn on the hand dryer. Set it to
warm temperature, not too hot, and a
gh speed. Work over the coat
suring that the airflow lifts the coat so
at warm air penetrates through to the
se of the coat and the skin.

Take care using the dryer around
e ears and eyes.

4

continued overleaf ▶

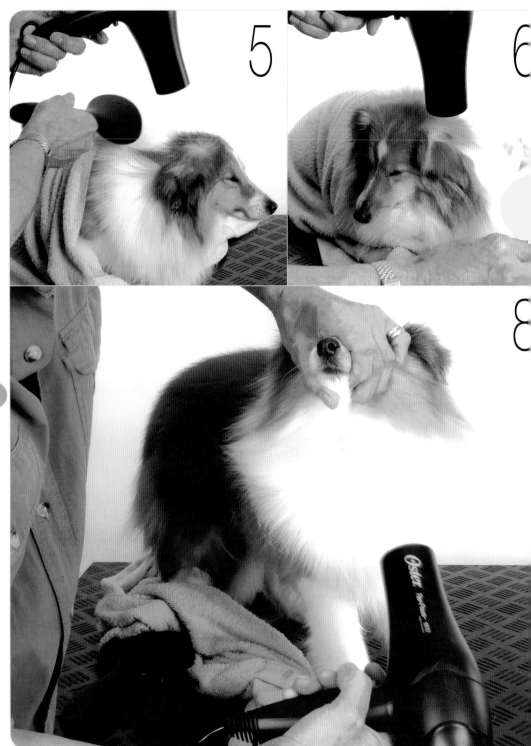

Use a slicker brush on the coat in conjunction with the dryer. Brush in the direction of hair growth and right down to the roots to get rid of loose hair.

Brush through the thick hair behind the ears and around the ruff.

The picture shows how the airflow lifts the coat to expose the undercoat.

Hold the muzzle to keep the head still and protect the eyes while you dry the chest and under the neck.

Finish off with a gentle comb through the coat – job done.

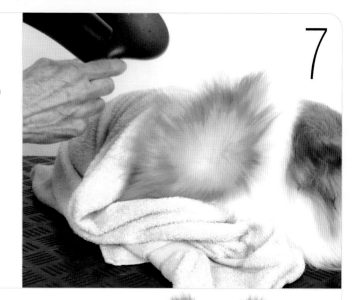

7

9

BATHING AND DRYING

Preparation: First, make sure you have to hand all the equipment that you require before starting: towels, shampoo etc. All pre-bath work should be done at your grooming station. It is important to keep to a regular pattern, which will make you and your pet feel more secure about the process. Check the ears to see if they need cleaning. Use an ear wipe if necessary and then plug each ear with cotton wool to stop water getting in. (And do remember to remove the cotton wool after the bath!).

• Before you start bathing, make sure you have gone over the entire body to remove any serious mats or tangles. If you know how to do so competently, pluck any long hair inside the ear canal, using ear powder and your fingers. Do not delve into the ear – just pluck what you can reach comfortably. Use a shampoo and conditioner which are most suitable for your dog. Shampoo very thoroughly, getting your fingers down to the base of the hair and getting a good lather and massage action going. After the first shampoo, most of the dirt will have been removed. Apply a second lather, then rinse. Apply your conditioner and leave it for a while so as to get maximum benefit from it. Then give the coat a final rinse.

• Towel dry gently: if you rub too hard or keenly you will just end up tangling and matting the hair. So start by blotting and gently rubbing the hair with a good thick towel until you have removed as much moisture as possible. Then dry with a hair dryer. This has to be done in a methodical way to make sure all areas are

reached. Blow the hair away from the body while using a moderately firm pin or slicker brush, in a similar way to blow-drying human hair. Lightly brush the area of the coat where the dryer is focused, with light, quick strokes going to the end of the hair shaft. Straighten the hair as you go and do not move on to the next section until the brush flows freely through the area of the coat you are currently working on.

• Do be careful not to scrape or scratch the skin with your brush. If you do, this can cause what is called brush burn which will be painful for the dog. So keep an eye on the skin and let the brush glide rather than digging or pulling it through the coat. After drying is finished, thoroughly groom through the coat with a comb.

COATS

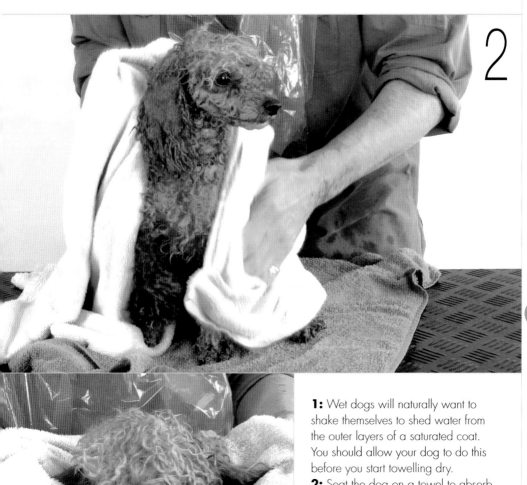

1: Wet dogs will naturally want to shake themselves to shed water from the outer layers of a saturated coat. You should allow your dog to do this before you start towelling dry.

2: Seat the dog on a towel to absorb moisture from the paws, rump and underside of the body and use a second towel to blot and pat the coat dry. Don't rub too hard or you risk creating tangles in the densely growing coat.

3: Gently dry the head with the towel. Pendulous ears can be dried by rubbing them gently with the towel between the fingers and thumbs of each hand.

continued overleaf ▶

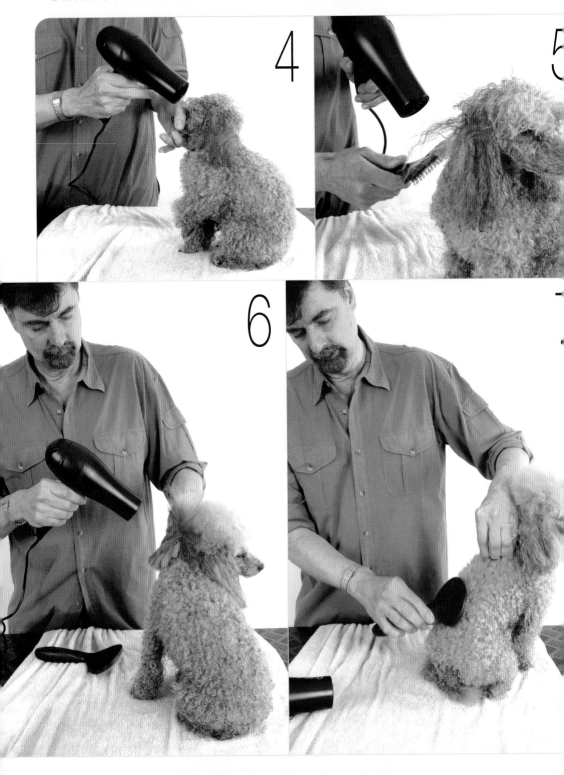

8

: Protect the eyes with one hand as you dry the head with a hair dryer.
, 6: Use light strokes of a slicker brush in conjunction with the dryer working on the ears and top knot.
: Then move onto the body and progress methodically. You can see how a wool coat fluffs up as it dries.
: Brush in all directions, even against the lie of the coat, as you move around the dog to ensure that the warm air gets right to the base of the coat.
: Comb through to complete.

9

continued overleaf ▶

USING A STAND DRYE

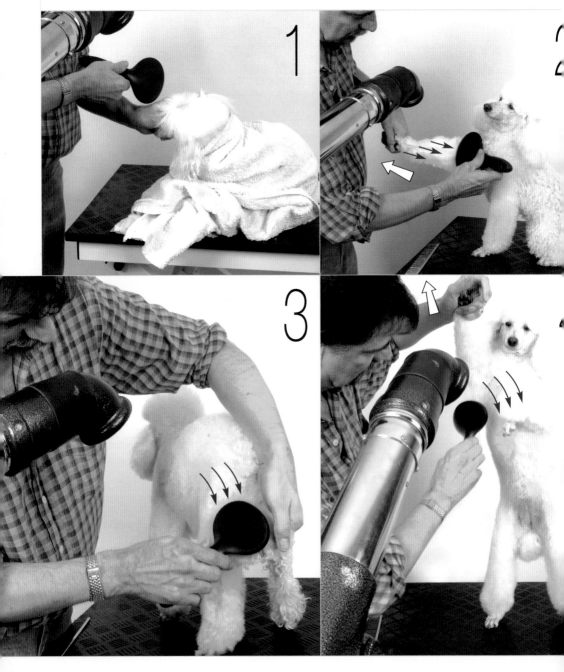

TAND DRYERS

he advantage of professional dryers
 that they leave both hands free to
anipulate the dog more easily.

: Start with the head, as before.

: You can stretch out the legs to
cker the hair on the front limbs.

: And support the rear quarters.

: It's very useful to be able to support
e dog as it stands on its hind legs so
at you can get at the chest and belly.

: Finish by thoroughly combing the
ead, ears and the entire body.

: You will be pleased with the result!

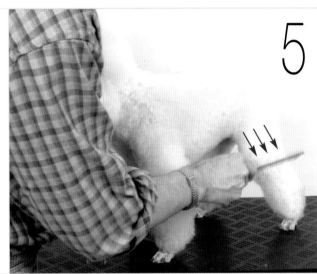

WIRE HAIRED COATS

BATHING AND DRYING

Preparation: First, make sure you have to hand all the equipment that you require before starting: towels, shampoo etc. All pre-bath work should be done at your grooming station. It is important to keep to a regular pattern, which will make you and your pet feel more secure about the process. Check the ears to see if they need cleaning. Use an ear wipe if necessary and then plug each ear with cotton wool to stop water getting in. (And do remember to remove the cotton wool after the bath!)

• Make sure that you have given the dog a thorough brush and comb through the coat to remove as much loose hair as possible. Use a quality, all-purpose shampoo unless another type of product is required. Get your fingers deeply into the coat, making sure that you massage the shampoo down to the roots of the hair everywhere, and especially in the thick hind breeches, the tail and around the collar ruff – in all these area the hair is especially thick and dense. Then thoroughly rinse until the dog is squeaky clean. Do not use a conditioner.

• Vigorously hand towel dry and then brush dry while working with a hair dryer until completely dry. Throughout the bathing and drying process, you will find that you get a lot of loose hair coming away. After drying is finished, groom through with a comb.

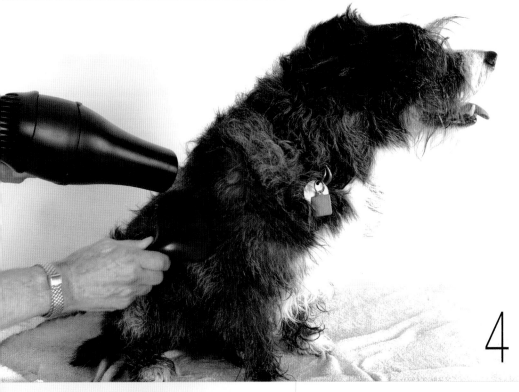

4

5

1: Start by towelling the head and front quarters. A second towel spread under the dog helps to absorb moisture.

2: Towel dry the underside. If your dog has a tendency to fidget, it may help to clip on his lead for extra control.

3: Dry the hind quarters and tail.

4: Then start using a slicker to brush out the coat under a warm airflow. This type of coat is quite tough and stiff and does not generally tangle much.

5: Move the dryer around the body, also using your fingers to raise the hair.

continued overleaf ▶

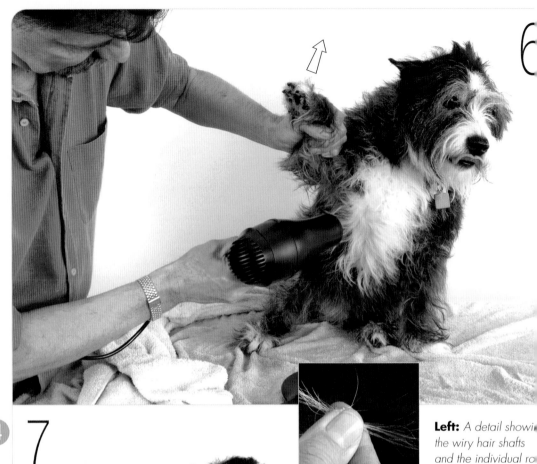

6

7

74

Left: *A detail showin[g]
the wiry hair shafts
and the individual ro[ot]
bulbs that come awa[y]
when hand stripped.*

6: Raise the front legs to direct warm
air at the friction areas underneath.
7: Work down the legs and
systematically around the body.
8: Once the coat is more or less dry,
comb through to remove any loose
hair. The comb should flow easily as
this coat tends not to harbour tangles.
9: Raise the head to allow you to
comb chest and neck areas. Don't
forget the beard and eyebrows.
10: A clean, dry dog – quite a
transformation!

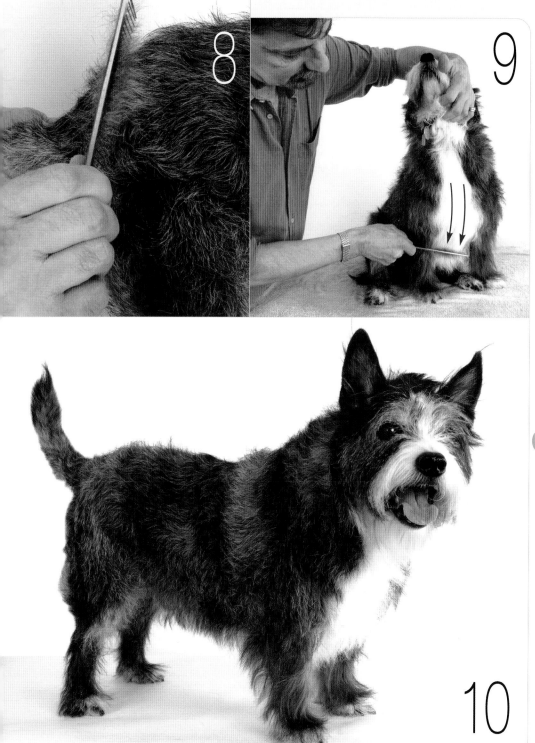

HAIRLESS TYPE

What Is The Coat Like?

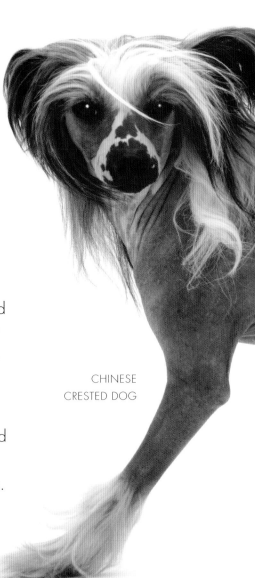

- There is a very small group of dogs that are not coated at all, except sometimes for small amounts of hair on top of the head and on the ears, feet and tail.

- The skin will need regular attention to keep it in optimum condition.

- These dogs are very susceptible to weather conditions. The skin will need the protection of sunscreen in summer to avoid sunburn. In winter, coats are required to maintain body warmth.

CHINESE
CRESTED DOG

- Skin maintenance includes regular oiling, but in some dogs this may lead to eruptions of blackheads. Only oil after bathing when the skin is dirt-free.

- Dental care is especially important with Chinese Crested as they have a tendency to lose teeth quite easily.

MEXICAN
HAIRLESS

CHINESE CRESTED

Toy Group
- Chinese Crested
- Peruvian Inca Orchid
  or Moonflower Dog

Utility Group
- Mexican Hairless

Bathing & Drying

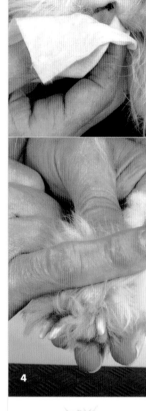

FREQUENCY

- Bathe ideally once a week to once to every four weeks.

PRE-BATH

- Put a plug of cotton wool gently in each ear to prevent water getting into the ear canal.

BATHING

- Use a gentle shampoo to cleanse the body, which can be prone to blackheads, and a tearless shampoo for the head. Only one application needed.
- Rinse off with clean water.

DRYING

- Towel dry all over.
- Finish off with a hand dryer set to warm on the furnishings.

1 BODY CHECKS

1: EARS Monitor ears for wax, and dirt and clean inside folds.
2: EYES Clean sticky deposits out of eyes wiping away from the eye towards the nose.
3: TEETH Check teeth and gums – these teeth need descaling.
4: FEET Check nails, condition of pads and hair growth on paws.

2 PAW CARE

5: The hair between these pads is overgrown. If left, mats will develop and can cause soreness.
6: Carefully trim away excess growth around and between the claws with round ended scissors.
7: The trimmed paw looks tidier.
8: Clip long nails. With white nails, it's easy to see the quick.

78

GROOMING KIT

BABY OIL
DOUBLE ENDED COMB
SCISSORS
PIN BRUSH
SLICKER BRUSH

BABY OIL To moisturise dry skin.
SCISSORS To trim excess hair.
PIN BRUSH This is kinder to the exposed skin than a slicker.
DOUBLE ENDED COMB Just used to tidy after the pin brush.
SLICKER BRUSH Useful on paws when hair has tangled.

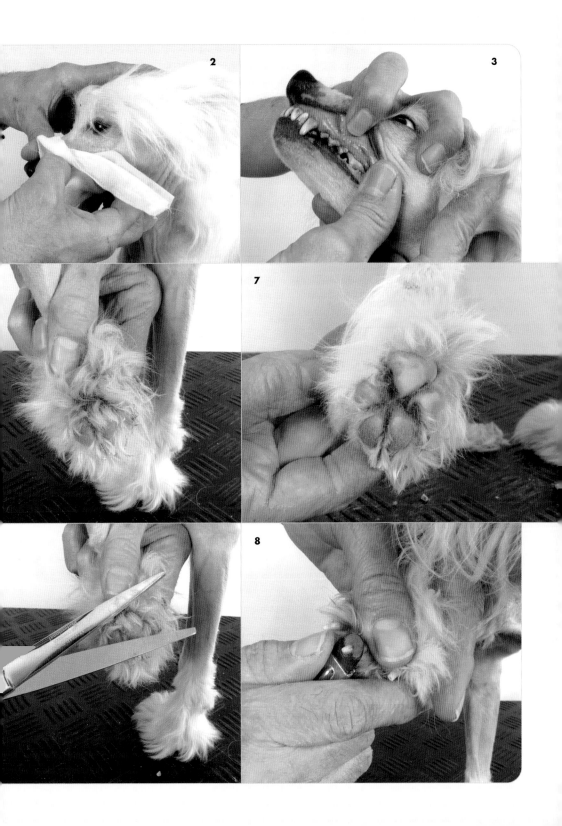

Brushing

1: Brush the hair on the head with a pin brush to ensure that it is free of tangles.

2: Follow up with a wide toothed comb. Comb carefully going with the natural flow of the hair.

3: Apply a little anti-static spray to the tail, then brush it gently with a pin brush.

4: Similarly use a slicker brush and then comb to tidy hair around the feet.

5: If the skin needs moisturising, massage a little baby oil into the body and legs.

6: This routine takes just a few minutes.

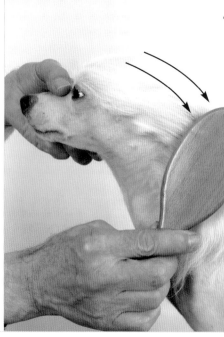

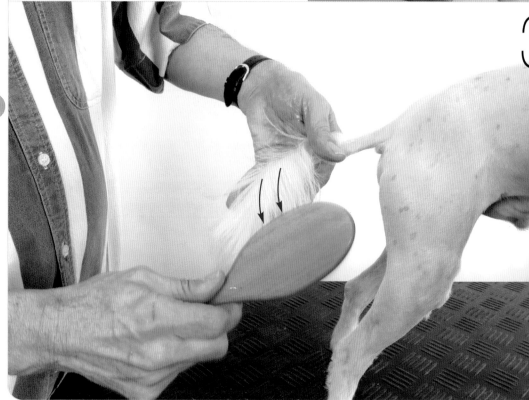

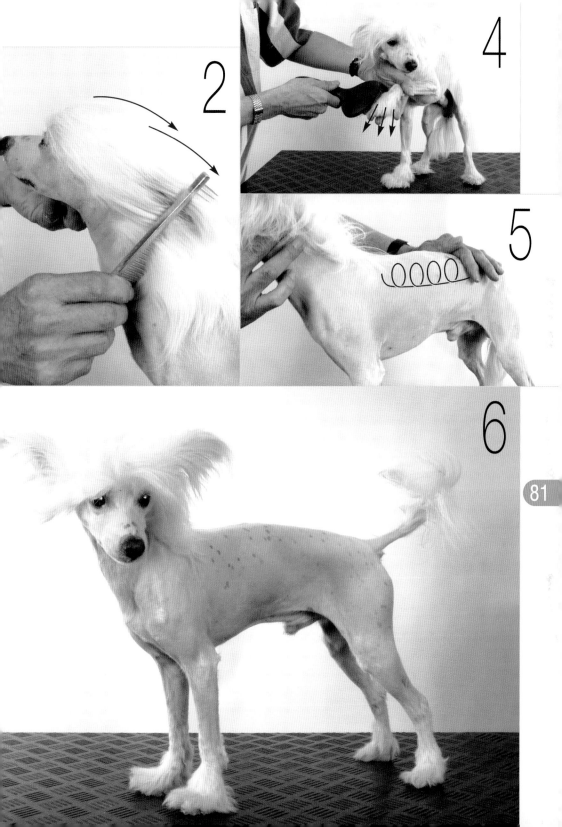

SMOOTH COATS

WHIPPET

What Is The Coat Like?

- Short single coat, lying close to the body.

- Coat does shed quite profusely so loose hairs accumulate on clothes, carpets and furnishings.

- Easy to maintain, generally clean, not liable to become smelly.

- These dogs tend to feel the cold, so may need the protection of a coat or jacket in winter.

- Coat provides little protection from insect stings or dog/cat bites.

- Take care with grooming tools as skin is soft and can be sensitive to harsh treatment.

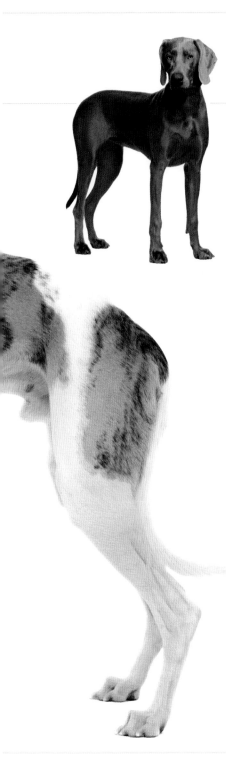

WEIMARANER

Gundog Group
- German Shorthaired Pointer
- Hungarian Vizsla
- Pointer
- Weimaraner

Hound Group
- Basenji
- Dachshund
- Greyhound
- Ibizan Hound
- Pharaoh Hound
- Whippet

BASENJI

Terrier Group
- Manchester Terrier
- Miniature Bull Terrier
- Staffordshire Bull Terrier

Toy Group
- Chihuahua – smooth
- English Toy Terrier
- Italian Greyhound
- Miniature Pinscher

DALMATIAN

Utility Group
- Boston Terrier
- Bulldog
- Dalmatian
- French Bulldog
- Shar Pei

Working Group
- Boxer
- Bullmastiff
- Dobermann
- Great Dane
- Mastiff

Bathing & Drying

FREQUENCY
- Bathe from once a week to once to every 12 weeks.

PRE-BATH
- Collect all items that you will need: cotton wool for blocking ears; shampoo and conditioner; jug for mixing shampoo; jug for rinsing the dog clean; towels.
- Place dog on an anti-slip mat in the bath.
- Put a plug of cotton wool gently in each ear to prevent water getting into the ear canal.

BATHING
- Make sure that the water temperature is suitable – just around warm.
- Throughly wet the dog all over except for the head.
- Use a quality, regular, all-purpose shampoo and massage the lather thoroughly into all parts of the body.
- Rinse most of the lather out of the coat.
- Now wash the dog's head with tear-free shampoo.
- Rinse whole dog thoroughly until coat is "squeaky clean".

DRYING
- See also pages 52-55 for more detailed illustrated advice about drying this type of coat.
- Start by towelling dry as much of the head and body as possible.
- Follow this by using a hand dryer over the body. Test the temperature of the airflow – it should be warm, not hot, and set to high speed. Be careful using the dryer around the head area.
- Use your hands or a bristle brush to raise the nap of the coat so that air can penetrate to the base of the hair.
- Work steadily until the coat is completely dry.

GROOMING KIT

BRISTLE BRUS

SHEEN BRUS

RUBBER BRUSH

**GROOMI
GLOVE**

USAGE
BRISTLE BRUSH A gentle brush for removing dead hair and dir
SHEEN BRUSH An alternative natural bristle brush that imparts a final shine to the coat.
RUBBER GLOVE Used to loosen and remove dead hair and dir and invigorate the skin.
RUBBER BRUSH Similar in action to the rubber glove – the rubbe tines stimulate the skin.

1 DOG CONTROL

- If your dog is liable to shy and you cannot secure him with a collar and lead, enlist the aid of a helper to hold the dog's head steady and thereby gain control.
- You want to prevent the dog from moving around or jumping off the grooming station.

2 BODY CHECKS

1: FEET Check the length of nails, condition of pads and clear any dirt from between the claws.

2: TEETH Check teeth and gums looking for tartar, signs of disease or inflammation.

3: EYES Check the eyes and clean out any sticky deposits.

4: EARS Monitor ears for wax, general dirt or signs of ear mites.

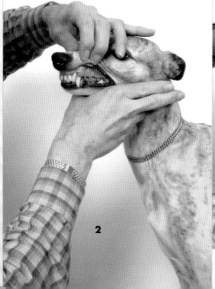

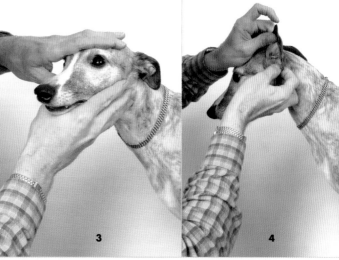

Brushing Sequence

1: Begin by using the bristle brush to remove dead hair and debris from the coat. By starting at the head, you gain instant control over the dog. Take care when working the brush around the eyes and ears.

2: Use a light but firm action with the brush. By raising the muzzle, you stretch out any wrinkles in the skin of the neck, so making it easier to brush there effectively.

3: You can use quite long strokes of the brush on a short coat as there will be little natural resistance to the flow of the brush's bristles across the surface of the skin.

4: Finish off over the rump and tail area. When working on the legs, it can help to raise individual legs; this effectively immobilises the dog and helps to stop it trying to move around on the table top.

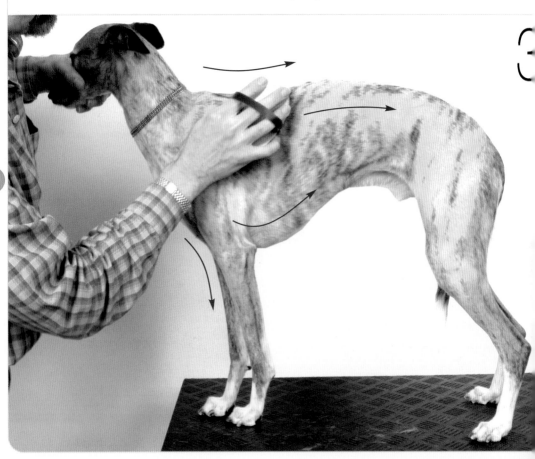

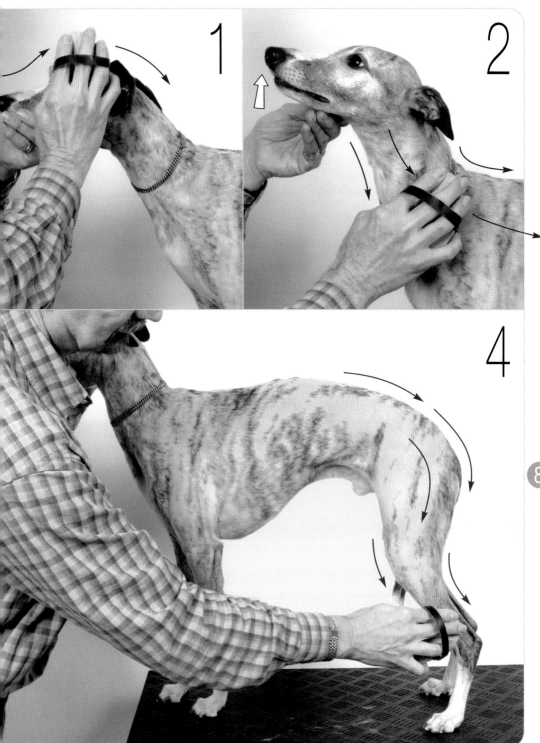

continued overleaf ▶

Grooming Glove Finish

1: Lift the head to make the skin taut and work the rubber grooming glove over the neck and chest area.

2: To remove loose hair you should work to and fro in circular fashion across the body. You can use quite long strokes. The rubber pimples on the glove "embrace" the coat and stimulate the skin. The effect for the dog is not unlike a stimulating body massage.

3: Work systematically along the flanks. With this sort of coat you can work in any direction with the glove. You should lift each leg to work the mitt under the armpits.

4: Complete the job by working on the other side of the dog. It may help the dog if you support the limb you are working on. It puts you in quiet, but strong, control.

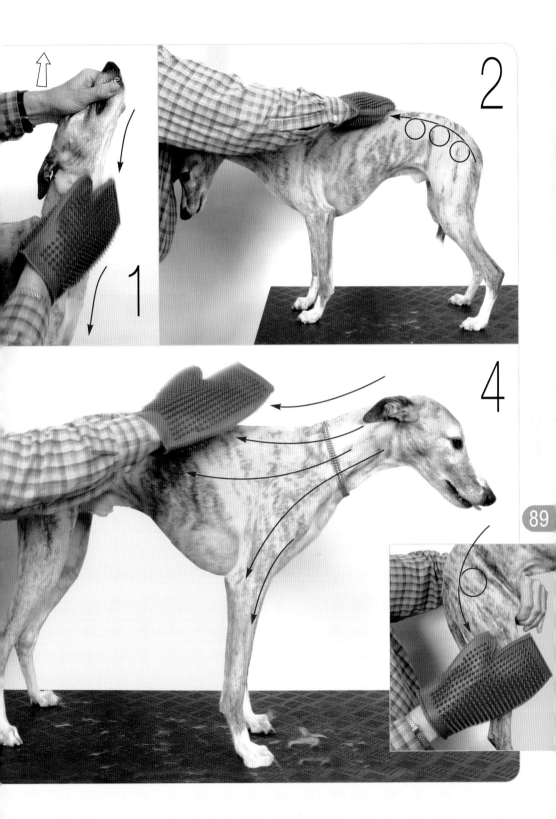

SHORT COATS

What Is The Coat Like?

- Short coat, lying close to the body, with another very short coat underneath. Harsher to the touch than a smooth coat.

- Coat is generally dense and quite water-resistant – helps to protect the dog.

- The coat produces an oil, which may cause some dogs to become rather smelly.

- Coat tends to shed hair which can easily work its way into carpets, furnishings etc.

- Dog will require a fair amount of maintenance grooming, particularly at moulting times.

PUG

Gundog Group
- Labrador Retriever

Hound Group
- Basset Hound
- Beagle
- Bloodhound
- Rhodesian Ridgeback

Terrier Group
- Bull Terrier
- Fox Terrier (short coated)

Toy Group
- Griffon Bruxellois (short coated)
- Pug

Working Group
- Rottweiler

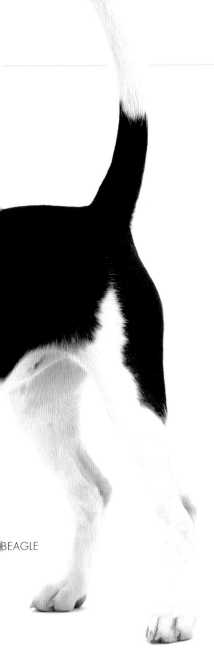

BEAGLE

LABRADOR RETRIEVER

Bathing & Drying

FREQUENCY
- Bathe from once a week to once to every 12 weeks.

PRE-BATH
- Collect all items that you will need: cotton wool for blocking ears; shampoo and conditioner; jug for mixing shampoo; jug for rinsing the dog clean; towels.
- Place dog on an anti-slip mat in the bath.
- Put a plug of cotton wool gently in each ear to prevent water getting into the ear canal.

BATHING
- Make sure that the water temperature is suitable – just around warm.
- Throughly wet the dog all over except for the head.
- Use a quality, regular, all-purpose shampoo and massage the lather thoroughly into all parts of the body.
- Rinse most of the lather out of the coat.
- Now wash the dog's head with tear-free shampoo.
- Rinse whole dog thoroughly until coat is "squeaky clean".

DRYING
- See also pp 52-55 for more detailed illustrated advice about drying this type of coat.
- Start by towelling dry as much of the head and body as possible.
- Then use a hand dryer over the body. The temperature of the airflow should be warm, not hot, and set to high speed. Be careful using the dryer around the head area.
- Use your hands or a bristle brush to raise the nap of the coat so that air can penetrate to the base of the hair.
- Work steadily until the coat is completely dry.

GROOMING KIT

GROO
GLOV

BRISTLE BRUSH

DOUBLE
ENDED COME

SLICKER B

USAGE
BRISTLE BRUSH "Kinder" than a slicker, useful to remove mud
SLICKER BRUSH Used for initia all-over body groom.
COMB Fine toothed comb used principally over the body.
GROOMING GLOVE For finishir off all over the body.

BASSET HOUND

92

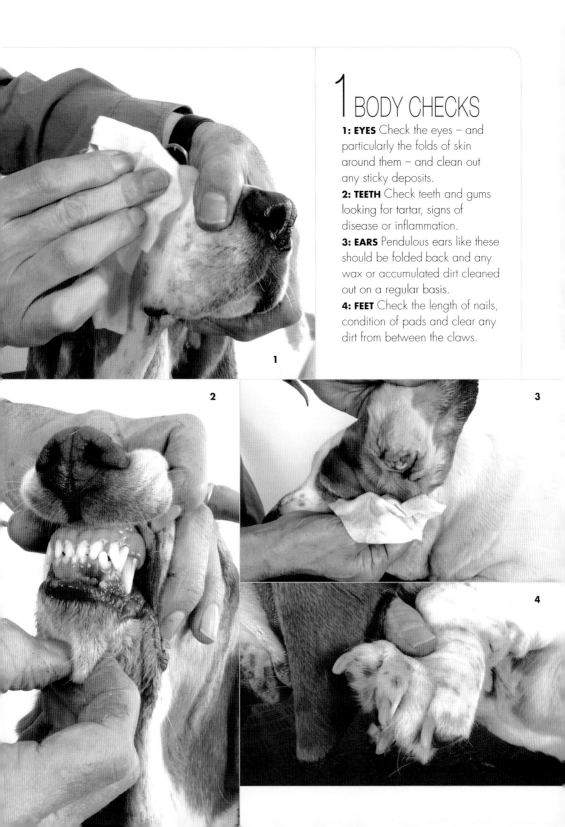

1 BODY CHECKS

1: EYES Check the eyes – and particularly the folds of skin around them – and clean out any sticky deposits.

2: TEETH Check teeth and gums looking for tartar, signs of disease or inflammation.

3: EARS Pendulous ears like these should be folded back and any wax or accumulated dirt cleaned out on a regular basis.

4: FEET Check the length of nails, condition of pads and clear any dirt from between the claws.

Removing Dried Mud

1: If your dog is muddy, use a bristle brush to clean off mud – it is less abrasive than a slicker.

2: Pay attention to any folds of skin; you are aiming to clear specks of mud not loose hair.

3: Brush the underside of low-slung dogs like this.

Brushing Sequence

4: For maintenance grooming, use the slicker all over the body. Start at the head and raise the muzzle to tauten normally slack areas of skin.

5: Lifting a front leg is a useful way of gaining control over a fidgety dog. It is less inclined to move when one of its legs is off the ground.

6: The slicker brush is very effective at taking out plenty of loose coat. Even short coated dogs can shed quite profuse quantities of hair.

7: Work systematically along both flanks of the dog with the slicker. Ease up any loose folds of skin so that the brush gets everywhere.

8: Finish with the hind quarters and the areas around the tail. A stout tail like a Basset's provides a useful handle!

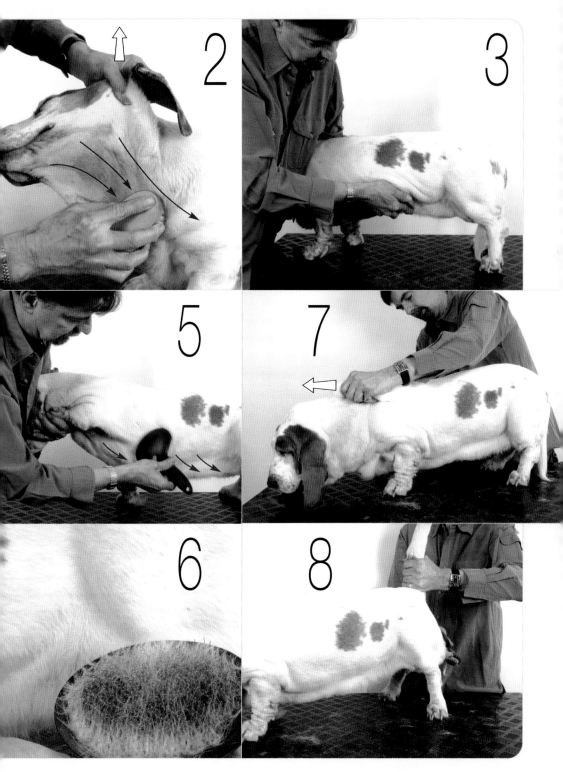

continued overleaf ▶

Combing

1: Follow the same brushing pattern when you come to comb the body. On a short coat, you can comfortably use the fine toothed end of the comb.

2: As you will not encounter any tangles in such a short coat, you can use quite long strokes of the comb along the body. The comb will continue to remove loose hair entwined in the coat.

3: The regular pattern in the texture of the coat shows how easy the combing action can be.

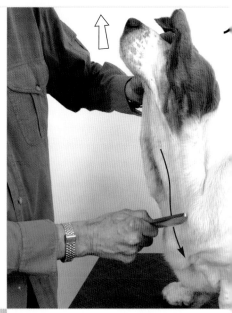

Finishing

4: A rubber grooming glove provides the finishing touches. Rub quite vigorously up and down the legs and use more circular actions over the body.

5: The loose hair lying on the table top shows how effective the glove is as a finishing tool.

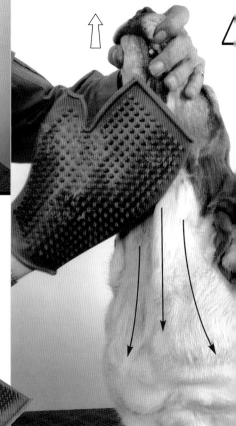

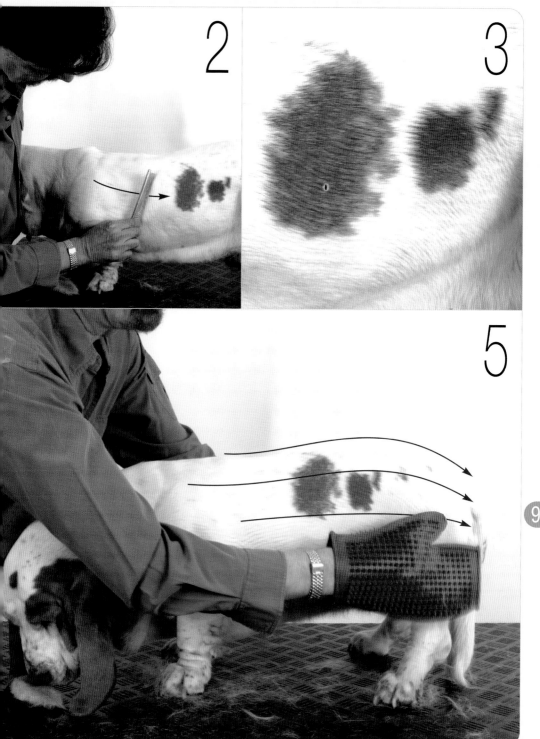

COMBINATION COATS

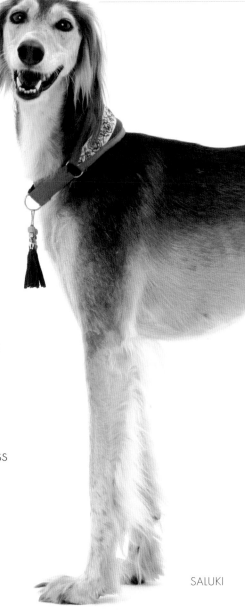

What Is The Coat Like?

- As the name suggests, coats of this type consist of a mix of a long flowing coat combined with a shorter, smoother one.

- Coat around the face and the front of the legs is short and tight. The body coat is a bit longer, while the furnishings on the underside, rear of the legs and tail are longer still.

- Care must be taken with the feet – the hair between the toes and pads can clump and tangle and trap grass seeds and other debris.

- Coat sheds quite a lot of hair in the moulting season.

- More maintenance grooming is needed as some of the hair is of sufficient length to tangle and mat.

SALUKI

COCKER SPANIEL

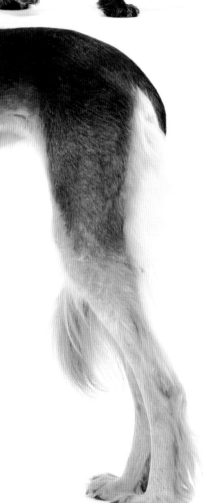

Gundog Group
- American Spaniel
- Clumber Spaniel
- Cocker Spaniel
- English Setter
- Field Spaniel
- Flat-coated Retriever
- Golden Retriever
- Gordon Setter
- Irish Setter
- Irish Red and White Setter
- Springer Spaniel
- Sussex Spaniel

Hound Group
- Borzoi
- Saluki

Toy Group
- Affenpinscher
- Cavalier King Charles Spaniel
- Japanese Chin
- King Charles Spaniel
- Papillon
- Pekingese

Utility Group
- Tibetan Spaniel

Working Group
- Leonberger

GOLDEN RETRIEVER

RED SETTER

Bathing & Drying

FREQUENCY

- Bathe from once a week to once to every 12 weeks.

PRE-BATH

- Collect all items that you will need: cotton wool for blocking ears; shampoo and conditioner; jug for mixing shampoo; jug for rinsing the dog clean; towels.
- Place dog on an anti-slip mat in the bath.
- Put a plug of cotton wool gently in each ear to prevent water getting into the ear canal.
- Before you start bathing, make sure that you brush over the entire body to remove any serious mats and tangles.

BATHING

- Make sure that the water temperature is suitable – just around warm.
- Throughly wet the dog all over except for the head.
- Use a quality, regular, all-purpose shampoo and massage the lather thoroughly into all parts of the body, especially under the front legs, around the back of the ears, breeches and groin, and along the stomach.

- Rinse the lather thoroughly out of the coat.
- Now wash the dog's head with tear-free shampoo.
- Apply a suitable conditioner on the fringing at the back of the legs, shirt front, stomach, rear of hind legs and tail fringes. Leave on for as long as directed in the instructions to gain maximum benefit.
- Rinse whole dog thoroughly until coat is "squeaky clean".

DRYING

- See also pp 56–61 for more detailed illustrated advice about drying this type of coat.
- Start by vigorously towelling dry as much as possible. Brush hair with flow of the coat, ensuring that longer fringe hair is tangle-free.
- Then use a hand dryer over the body. The temperature of the airflow should be warm, not hot, and set to high speed. Be careful using the dryer around the head area.
- Brush in the direction that the coat grows to allow it to lie close to the skin.
- When dry, groom through the coat with a comb.

GROOMING KIT

WIDE TOOTHED COMB

SLICKER BRUSH

USAGE

SLICKER BRUSH The slicker is used for the initial work, and should be used to gently brush out any tangles.

WIDE TOOTHED COMB Follow up with a wide toothed comb ensuring that you cover the whole body methodically.

1-3: FEET Check nails (trim if necessary), the condition of pads and clear dirt from between the claws. The coat here has a tendency to mat so neatly trim the hair if it is long.

4: TEETH Check teeth and gums for tartar or inflammation.

5: EARS Overhanging ears like these should be folded back and wax or dirt cleaned out.

6: EYES Check the eyes and clean out any sticky deposits.

Brushing Sequence

1: Start at the head with the slicker brush. This engage[s] you with the dog immediately. Lift the muzzle to stretch the skin of the neck to assist the flow of the brush.

2: Continue working along the body where the coat is longer and silkier. Brush with the flow of the hair in sho[rt] sweeps. If you encounter any tangles, brush them gentl[y] out, starting at the outside of the mat and working dow[n] towards the roots of the hair.

3: Brush the underleg furnishings. The brush will pull ou[t] quite a lot of loose hair (inset). Use fairly short strokes working with the lie of the hair. Make sure that the brus[h] passes right through the full extent of the coat.

4: Lift the front leg to allow the leg furnishings to fall in[to] an uninterrupted curtain of hair. It is easier to brush it th[at] way than when the feathering is lying tight to the leg.

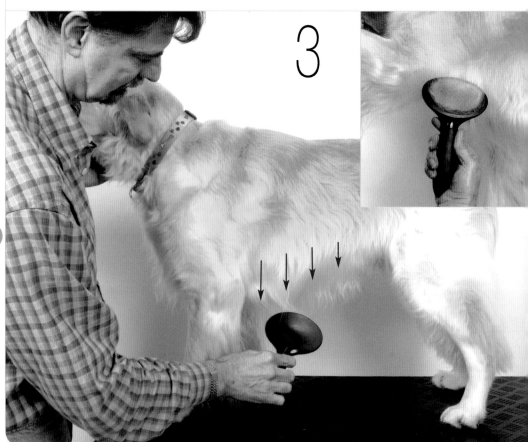

3

continued overleaf ▶

Brushing Sequence

5: Pay close attention to the friction areas under the legs and near the tail, as they can harbour tangles.

6: When brushing the featherings on the hind legs, it helps to use your other hand as a support for the hair. This stops the brush pulling directly on the dog's skin.

7: The tail and breeches are always heavily coate Lift the tail to get access to the breeches and work systematically bit by bit to get right down to the root.

8: Lifting the tail allows the prolific coat to cascade in a downward curtain. This is easier to brush than if you try to work along the tail as it hangs naturally.

9: You will often find a lot of hair trapped in the brush

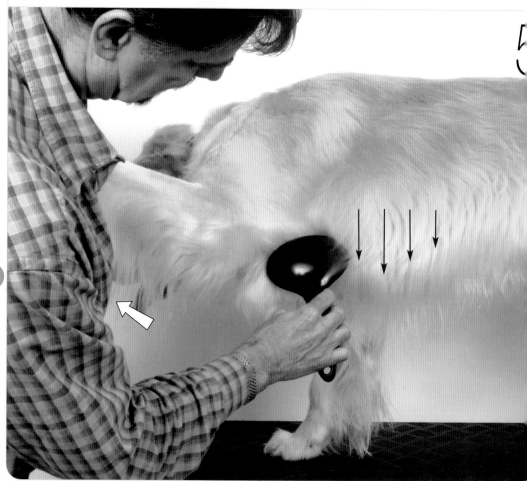

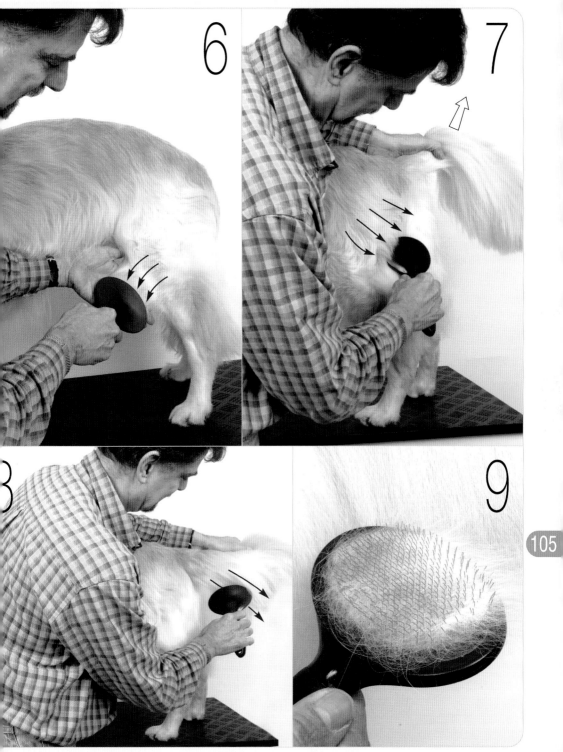

continued overleaf ▶

Combing Finish

1: Start to comb behind the ears and under the neck.

2: As you are unlikely to encounter tangles, you can use longer strokes with the comb than you do with the slicker. Aim to comb in comfortable sweeps.

3: Work along the flanks of the body and round the hindquarters and rump.

4: Also gently comb the feathering under the stomach.

5: Lift the legs to allow you to comb out the leg furnishings as they fall towards the ground.

6: Lift the tail to get at the breeches and then comb the feathering on the tail itself. Then either turn the dog or move round to the other side to repeat the process.

7: The whole job should only take 10-15 minutes.

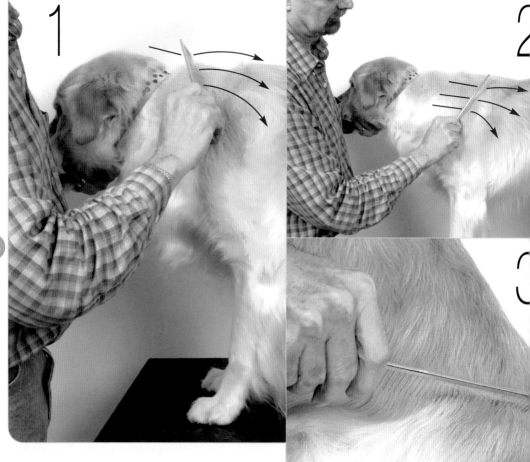

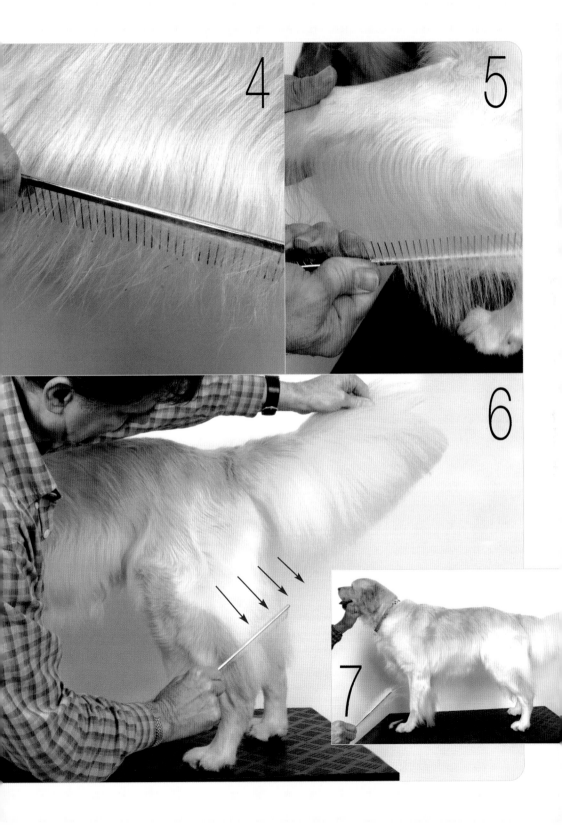

DOUBLE COATS

What Is The Coat Like?

- Depending on the breed the coat is a combination of very short, short to moderate and moderate to long hair.

- The outer guard coat feels quite tough and harsh while the profuse soft undercoat is thick. Dogs with this type of coat can tolerate quite severe weather conditions.

- Coat around face and on front of legs is short and tight.

- There is a noticeable seasonal shedding pattern. If not cleared, the loose, moulted hair will tangle and mats and clumps will form.

- The coat naturally produces an oil, which may cause some dogs to become rather smelly.

POMERANIAN

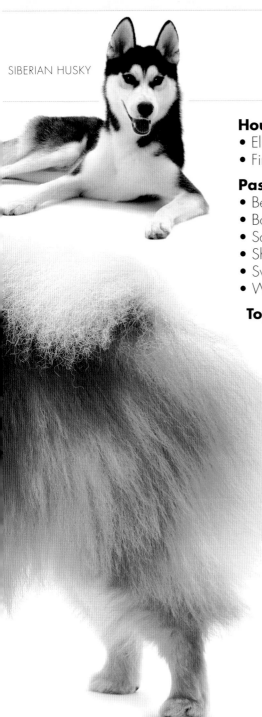

SIBERIAN HUSKY

Hound Group
- Elkhound
- Finnish Spitz

Pastoral Group
- Belgian Shepherd Dog
- Border Collie
- Samoyed
- Shetland Sheepdog
- Swedish Vallhund
- Welsh Corgi

Toy Group
- Pomeranian

Utility Group
- Chow Chow
- German Spitz
- Japanese Akita
- Japanese Shiba Inu
- Japanese Spitz
- Keeshond
- Schipperke

Working Group
- Bernese Mountain Dog
- Newfoundland
- Siberian Husky
- St Bernard

BORDER COLLIE

WELSH CORGI

Bathing & Drying

FREQUENCY

- Bathe from once a week to every 12 weeks. Bathe more frequently when moulting.

PRE-BATH

- Collect all items that you will need: cotton wool for blocking ears; shampoo and conditioner; jug for mixing shampoo; jug for rinsing the dog clean; towels.
- Put a plug of cotton wool gently in each ear to prevent water getting into the ear canal.
- Before you start bathing, brush over the entire body to remove any mats and tangles. Pay special attention to the areas around the ears, the backs of the legs, the tail, and the chest and stomach.

BATHING

- Throughly wet the dog all over except for the head.
- Use a quality, regular, all-purpose shampoo and massage the lather thoroughly into all parts of the body, especially dense areas of hair.
- Rinse thoroughly.
- Now wash the dog's head with tear-free shampoo.

- Rinse whole dog thoroughly.
- Do not apply a conditioner to this type of coat.

DRYING

- See also pp 66-69 for more detailed illustrated advice.
- Towel dry vigorously, then use a hair dryer working in the direction of coat growth.
- Use a slicker brush to remove stubborn dead coat.
- When dry, groom through the coat with a comb.

GROOMING KIT

DOUBLE ENDED COMB

TRIMMING SCISSORS

SLICKER BRUSH

USAGE

SLICKER BRUSH Use a firm slicker brush so that you can get right down to the roots of the hair.
DOUBLE ENDED COMB For finishing off grooming the coat.
SCISSORS To trim excess hair.

1 BODY CHECKS

1: EYES Check the eyes and clean out any sticky deposits.
2: EARS Monitor ears for wax, and dirt and clean with a wip
3: FEET Check the length of na condition of pads and clear a dirt from between the claws.
4: TEETH Check teeth and gum

2 FOOT TRIM

5: Brush up long hair betweer the toes and trim carefully.
6: The result is a much tidier and better defined paw.
7: Any long hair growing on hocks should also be trimmed.
8: The finished job showing a untrimmed (above) and trimmed leg (below).

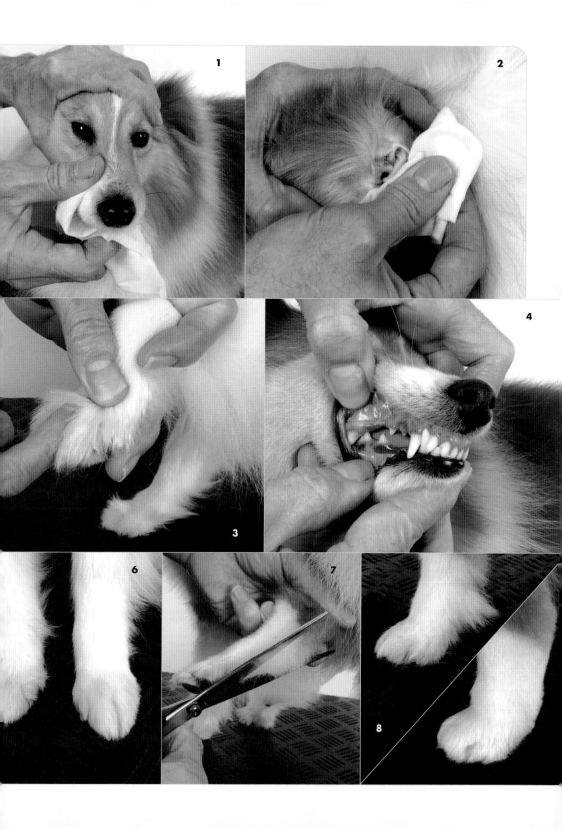

Brushing Sequence

1: When dealing with this type of coat, you must be methodical and work in lines along the body. Initially you must part the hair with a comb or your hand to expose the undercoat.

2: This picture shows the reason for line brushing. The top coat is raised with one hand to expose the undercoat which requires dedicated attention.

3: Now work along this line with a slicker brush. You must try to brush right down to the roots of the hair. If you don't raise the hair, you run the risk of the brush simply gliding through the top coat and not properly engaging with the undercoat which is where tangles and loose hair are found. You should brush along the line and then move up the body and repeat.

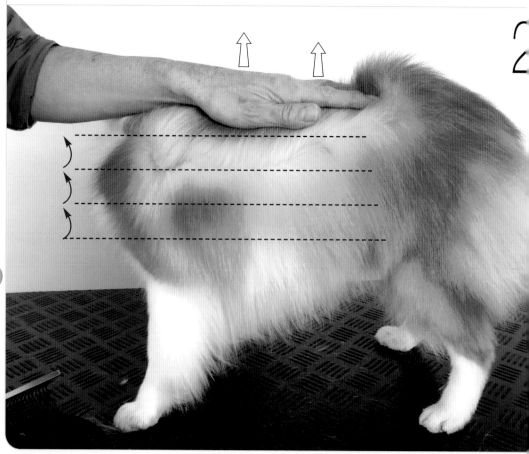

112

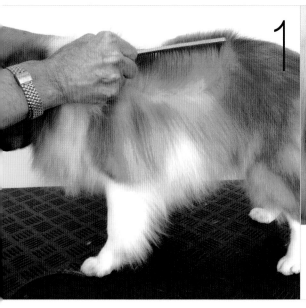

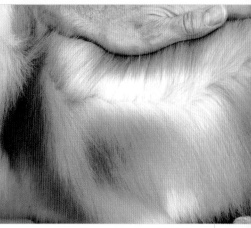

Above: The undercoat is the hair that moults and has a tendency to tangle and this is what you must brush out.

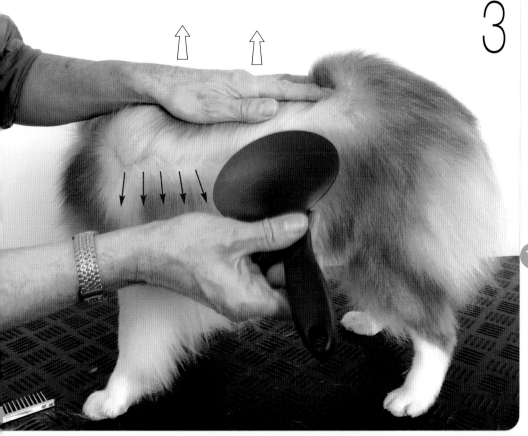

continued overleaf ▶

Finishing

1: Work systematically around head and neck.

2: Deal with the chest in a similar way.

3: Brush the sides of the tail and then lift it up so that you can tackle the underside.

4: The breeches often get tangled; lift the hair and brush it back down in an organised way working up the legs.

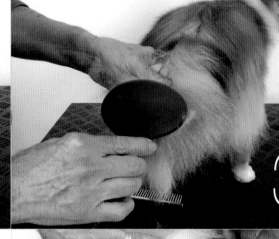

COMBING

5: Use a wide toothed comb to finish off and comb over the whole body. Comb the hair on the chest in both directions to ensure that all mats and tangles are eliminated.

6: Work along the lines of the body and pay attention to the friction points under the armpits and around the tail. Also check around the bottom for any soiling.

7: When finished the dog should look smart and alert – a tribute to your grooming skills.

114

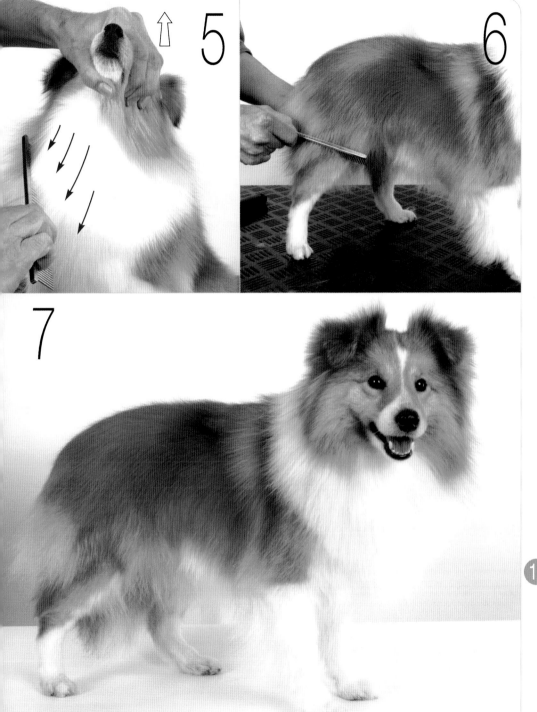

WOOL COATS

STANDARD POODLE

What Is The Coat Like?

- Considerable variation in coat types. Depending on the breed the coat is soft, curly, wavy or straight.

- A good choice for people who suffer from allergies as the coat is generally non-shedding/moulting.

- Coat grows continuously from all parts of the body.

- The coat will mat and tangle unless it is groomed on a very regular basis.

- Puppy coats are often quite fluffy and flyaway. Owners often bathe them frequently but they must ensure first that coat is tangle-free.

- A lot of dogs in this group are heavily trimmed for which you should seek professional assistance.

TOY POODLE

Gundog Group
- Irish Water Spaniel

Terrier Group
- Bedlington Terrier
- Kerry Blue Terrier
- Soft Coated
  Wheaten Terrier

Toy Group
- Bichon Frisé
- Bolognese
- Coton de Tulear

Utility Group
- Miniature Poodle
- Standard Poodle
- Toy Poodle

BICHON FRISE

COTON DE TULEAR

Bathing & Drying

FREQUENCY
- Bathe from once a week to once to every six weeks.

PRE-BATH
- Collect all items that you will need: cotton wool for blocking ears; shampoo and conditioner; jug for mixing shampoo; jug for rinsing the dog clean; towels.
- Place dog on an anti-slip mat in the bath.
- Put a plug of cotton wool gently in each ear to prevent water getting into the ear canal.
- Before you start bathing, make sure that you brush over the entire body to remove any serious mats and tangles.
- If you have been taught how to do so, pluck out by hand any long hair in the ear canal.

BATHING
- Make sure that the water temperature is suitable – just around warm.
- Throughly wet the dog all over except for the head.
- Use a quality, regular, all-purpose shampoo and massage the lather thoroughly into all parts of the body.

- Rinse most of the lather out of the coat.
- Apply a second lather, then rinse the shampoo out.
- Now wash the dog's head with tear-free shampoo.
- Apply a suitable conditioner and leave for 10 minutes to gain maximum benefit.
- Rinse whole dog thoroughly until coat is "squeaky clean".

DRYING
- See also pp 70-75 for more detailed illustrated advice about drying this type of coat.
- Start by towelling dry as much as possible. Don't rub too hard or you risk tangling the hair.
- Then use a hand dryer over the body. The temperature of th airflow should be warm, not h and set to high speed. Be careful using the dryer around the head area.
- Blow the hair away from the body using a moderately firm pin or slicker brush and workir on sections of the coat in the same way as drying human h
- Work methodically to make sure all areas of the dog are reached until the coat is dry.

GROOMING KIT

SLICKER BRUSH

USAGE
SLICKER BRUSH A slicker brush is needed to prevent the natur build-up of mats and tangles which this sort of coat is pron

1 BODY CHECKS

1: TEETH Check teeth and gums looking for tartar, or inflammation.

2: EYES Check the eyes and clean out any sticky deposits.

3: EARS Pendulous ears like these should be folded back and any wax or accumulated dirt cleaned out.

4: FEET Check the length of nails, condition of pads and clear any dirt from between the claws.

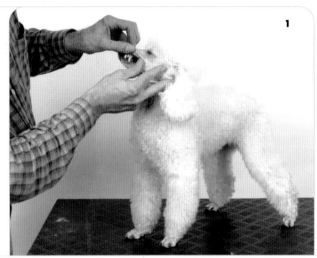

Trimming of wool coated dogs is usually undertaken by a professional.

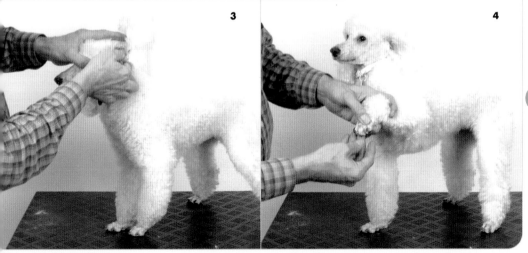

Brushing Sequence

1: When brushing wool coats, it is best to apply some anti-static spray. It lubricates the hair shafts and so make brushing this type of coat, which has a natural curl and a slight undercoat, considerably easier and gentler.

2: Hold the head steady and start by slicker brushing the top knot and the areas around the back of the head

3: Then move onto the ears holding each securely and brush with the lie of the hair to eliminate any tangles. Support the ear with your free hand to avoid tugging at the ear flap if resistance is met.

4: Stretch the front leg forward and brush against the lie of the hair from the top of the leg down. Only brush this way if the coat is short like this – on longer haired dogs brush with the lie of the coat

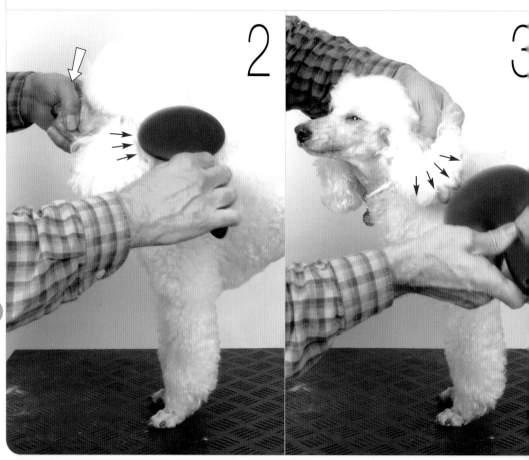

1

4

continued overleaf ▶

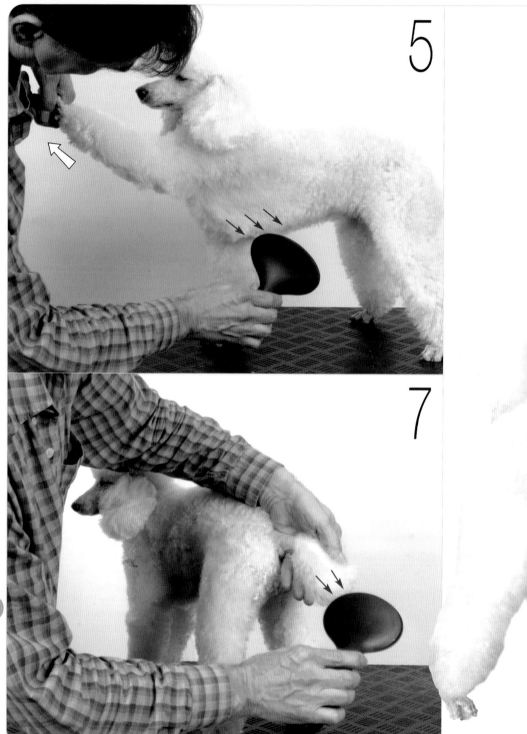

Finishing

Note on Combing

Wool coats tend to get tangly at the roots, and combing in these circumstances can pull on the dog's skin and cause discomfort. Ideally you should comb, as well as brush, the dog, but it is better to brush efficiently as shown, than engage in combing if the coat is clumpy and resistant.

5: Work over the body with the slicker brush. Lifting the leg like this helps to prevent the dog from moving about on the grooming table.

6: Thoroughly brush the friction areas under the legs where tangles can easily form.

7: Work methodically around the dog, brushing the chest and belly, rear quarters and tail, particularly if it has a pom-pom like this dog. Also check the breeches for signs of faecal soiling and trim away excess hair if necessary.

LONG HAIRED

What Is The Coat Like?

- These breeds grow a long, drop-type coat (meaning that it falls from the dog in a downward direction) over their entire body.

- If groomed to breed profile, the coats are left naturally long with just a little trimming around the feet, the anus and perhaps where the hair grows in front of the eyes.

- The vast majority of owners chose a shorter, more manageable trim for which you should seek professional assistance.

- The coat will certainly mat and tangle unless it is brushed very regularly, ideally three times a week or more.

- If not properly maintained, the coat will inevitably become very matted and may even need shaving off entirely to remedy the situation.

YORKSHIRE TERRIER

Hound Group
- Afghan Hound

Pastoral Group
- Bearded Collie
- Briard
- Old English Sheepdog

Terrier Group
- Australian Silky Terrier
- Skye Terrier

Toy Group
- Löwchen
- Maltese Terrier
- Yorkshire Terrier

Utility Group
- Lhasa Apso
- Shih Tzu
- Tibetan Terrier

LHASA APSO

BEARDED COLLIE

Bathing & Drying

FREQUENCY
- Bathe from once a week to once to every eight weeks.

PRE-BATH
- Collect all items that you will need: cotton wool for blocking ears; shampoo and conditioner; jug for mixing shampoo; jug for rinsing the dog clean; towels.
- Place dog on an anti-slip mat in the bath.
- Put a plug of cotton wool gently in each ear to prevent water getting into the ear canal.
- Before you start bathing, make sure that you brush over the entire body to remove any serious mats and tangles.

BATHING
- Make sure that the water temperature is suitable. Throughly wet the dog all over except for the head.
- Use a quality, regular, all-purpose shampoo and massage the lather thoroughly into all parts of the body.
- Rinse out most of the lather.
- Apply a second lather, then rinse the shampoo out.
- Now wash the dog's head

with tear-free shampoo.
- Apply a suitable conditioner and leave for 10 minutes to gain maximum benefit.
- Rinse whole dog thoroughly until coat is "squeaky clean".

DRYING
- See also pp 70-75 for more detailed illustrated advice about drying this type of coat.
- Start by towelling dry as much as possible. Don't rub too hard or you risk tangling the hair.
- Then use a hand dryer over the body. The temperature of the airflow should be warm, not hot, and set to high speed.
- Blow the hair away from the body using a moderately firm pin or slicker brush and working on sections of the coat in the same way as drying human hair.
- Work methodically to make sure all areas of the dog are reached until the coat is completely dry.

AFGHAN HOUND

GROOMING KIT

ANTI-STATIC SPRAY

WIDE TOOTHED COMB

PIN BRUSH

SLICKER BRUSH

USAGE
ANTI-STATIC SPRAY
PIN BRUSH Gentler than a slick but you must be very thorough.
SLICKER BRUSH Use on prolific coats. Good for friction areas.
WIDE TOOTHED COMB Finish by combing all over the body.

1 BODY CHECKS
1: TEETH Check teeth and gums
2: EYES Check the eyes and cl out any sticky deposits.
3: EARS Pendulous ears should folded back and cleaned caref
4 AND 5: FEET Check the lengt nails, condition of pads and cl any dirt from between the clav

Brushing Sequence

1: Anti-static spray makes grooming long haired dogs easier as it coats the hair shafts with lubrication.

2: A pin brush is gentler than a slicker, particularly when working around the eyes and ears. On a dog like this Bearded Collie, the fringing around the face and neck needs careful brushing.

3: Then move onto to the legs. Use your spare hand to support the leg. It also helps to control the dog.

4: Work from the bottom of the leg upwards. Brush the lower hair thoroughly, and when that section is completed move further up the leg.

5: Hold the hair above the section you are grooming out of the way, and proceed layer by layer along the body once the leg is done.

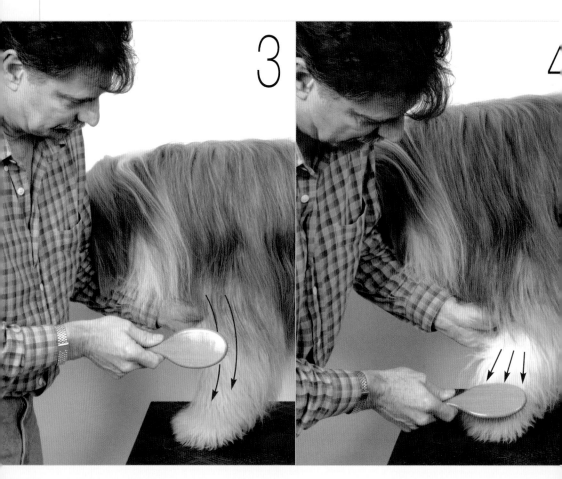

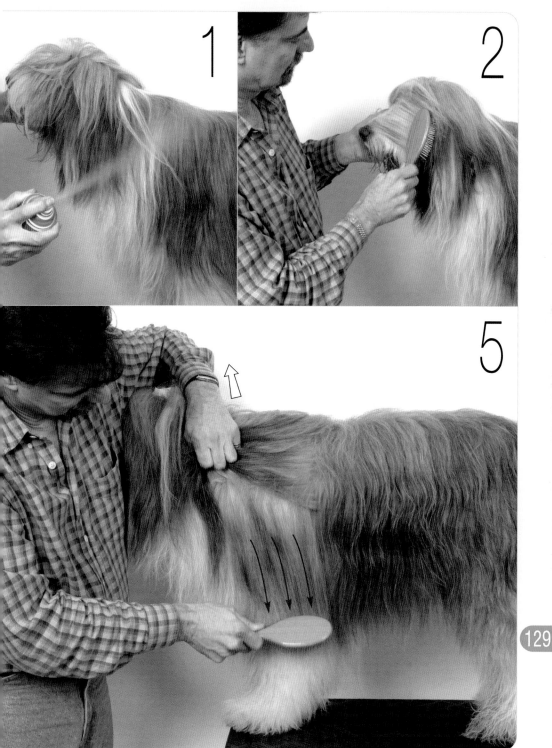

129

continued overleaf ▶

Finishing Sequence

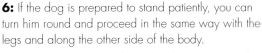

6: If the dog is prepared to stand patiently, you can turn him round and proceed in the same way with the legs and along the other side of the body.

7: If you can train your dog to lie down, so much the better as this is more comfortable, particularly for a bi dog. Use a slicker brush on friction areas under the le

8: Use the same line by line layering technique to bru the hair on the lower abdomen. In this position you co also access the stomach and chest areas.

9: Finally work all over the coat with the wide tooth comb. Comb the back line while the dog is standing up and then carefully comb the head

10: Long haired dogs do need a lot of maintenanc grooming – at least three times a week – but with regular attention, they will look impressive.

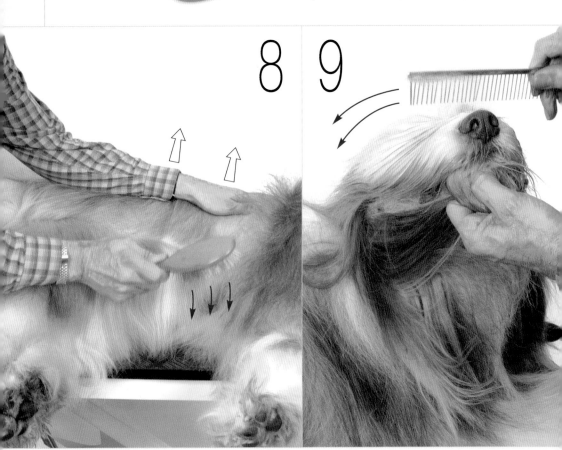

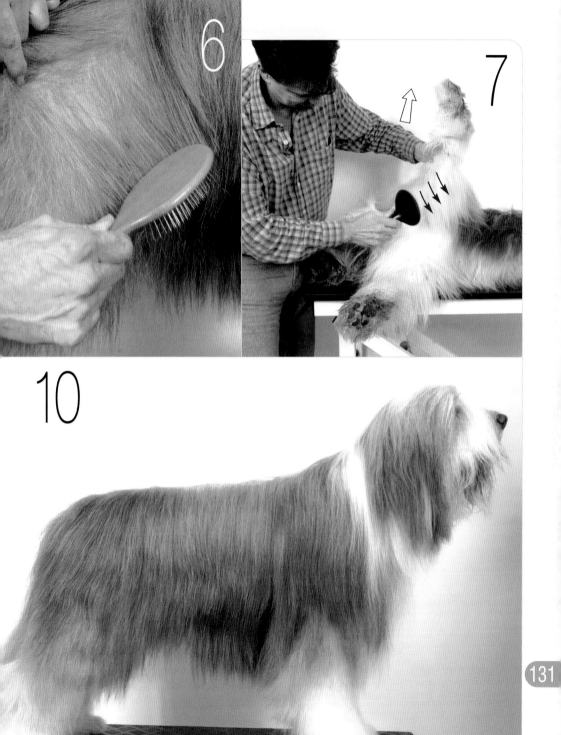

WIRE HAIRED

STANDARD SCHNAUZER

What Is The Coat Like?

- Combines a short, soft undercoa with wiry guard hairs growing through it to create a harsh, wiry and weatherproof jacket.

- The coat will require regular stripping or trimming.

- Trimming or stripping is quite complicated and breed-specific. The majority of breeds in this group are professionally trimmed to show them at their best.

- The coat requires regular maintenance grooming, especially in the moulting season. Although quite short, it can forr mats and tangles if not groomed.

- Special care should be taken with the feet as a lot of terrier breeds get mud and dirt between their pads which can cause discomfort, and even cysts.

REDALE TERRIER

CAIRN TERRIER

Terrier Group
- Airedale Terrier
- Australian Terrier
- Border Terrier
- Cairn Terrier
- Irish Terrier
- Jack Russell Terrier (wire haired)
- Lakeland Terrier
- Norfolk Terrier
- Norwich Terrier
- Scottish Terrier
- Sealyham Terrier
- Welsh Terrier
- West Highland White Terrier

Toy Group
- Griffon Bruxellois (rough coated)

Utility Group
- Giant Schnauzer
- Miniature Schnauzer
- Standard Schnauzer

WIRE HAIRED JACK RUSSELL TERRIER

Bathing & Drying

FREQUENCY

- Bathe from once a week to once to every 12 weeks.

PRE-BATH

- Collect all items that you will need: cotton wool for blocking ears; shampoo and conditioner; jug for mixing shampoo; jug for rinsing the dog clean; towels.
- Place dog on an anti-slip mat in the bath.
- Put a plug of cotton wool gently in each ear to prevent water getting into the ear canal.

BATHING

- Make sure that the water temperature is just around warm.
- Throughly wet the dog all over except for the head.
- Use a quality, regular, all-purpose shampoo and massage the lather deeply into the coat, especially the thick hind breeches, tail and collar ruff.
- Rinse most of the lather out of the coat.
- Now wash the dog's head with tear-free shampoo.
- Do not use a conditioner.
- Rinse whole dog thoroughly. until coat is "squeaky clean".

DRYING

- See also pages 62-65 for more detailed illustrated advice about drying this type of coat.
- Start by vigorously towelling dry as much of the head and body as possible.
- Follow this by using a hand dryer while brushing until completely dry. A lot of loose hair will come away. Finish by combing through when dry.

DOUBLE ENDED COMB

ROUND ENDED SCISSORS

SLICKER BRUSH

USAGE

SLICKER BRUSH A wire coat is harsh so a slicker is the most effective brush to use on it.
SCISSORS For trimming away excess hair around eyes, top knot and muzzle.
COMB Follow-up finishing tool.

1 BODY CHECKS

1: EYES Check the eyes and clean out any sticky deposits.
2: TEETH Check teeth and gums
3: EARS Monitor ears for wax, and dirt and clean with a wipe
4: FEET Check the length of nail condition of pads and clear an dirt from between the claws

2 BOTTOM TRIM

5: Profuse hair growth around tail means that wire haired dog can suffer soiling in this area.
6: Very carefully trim away excess hair from above the anu
7: And below the anus also.
8: To leave a neat result.

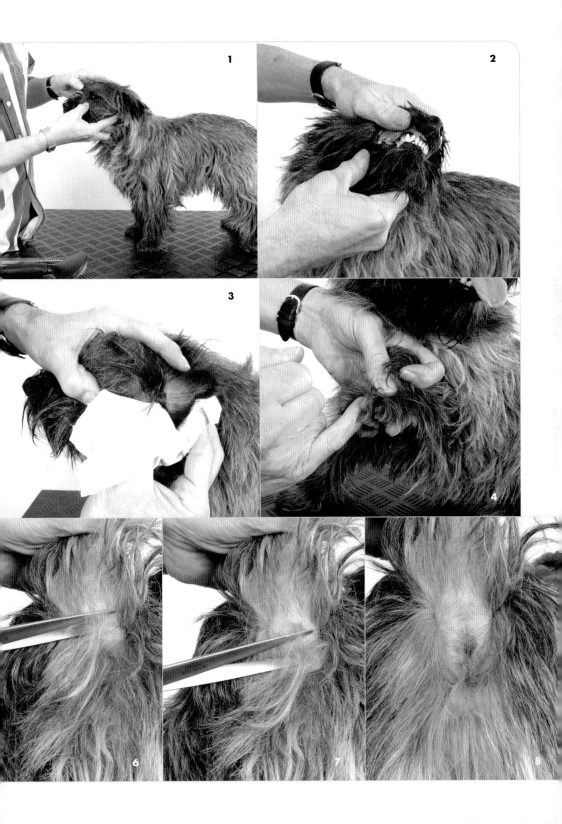

Brushing Sequence

1: Begin at the rear of the dog and apply some anti-static spray to help the brush slide through what is quite a resistant coat.

2: Using your other hand to support the rear leg, work down the leg and over the rear quarters with the slicker. In general, brush in the direction that the hair grows, working line by line up the body.

3: Anchor the tail with one hand and, after applying a little anti-static spray, brush out the hair against the supporting fingers.

4: Follow up with the wide-toothed comb to eliminate tangles.

5: Grip both front legs with one hand and raise the dog to allow you to work over the chest and stomach with a slicker brush and then comb.

6: Tilt the head back to expose the upper chest and neck and brush thoroughly here.

7: Brush around the head taking particular care to work on the friction areas behind the ears which have a tendency to harbour tangles.

Above: Use a comb to clean hair out of the slicker, always working in the direction that the pins lie to avoid twisting or breaking them.

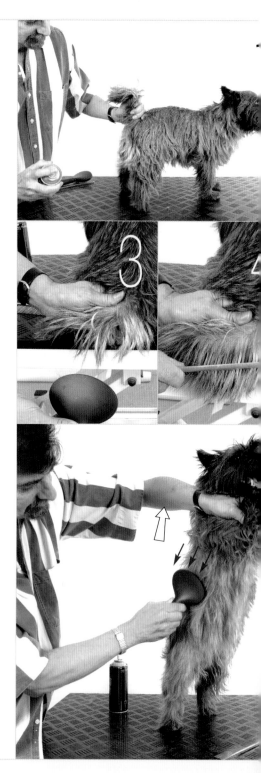

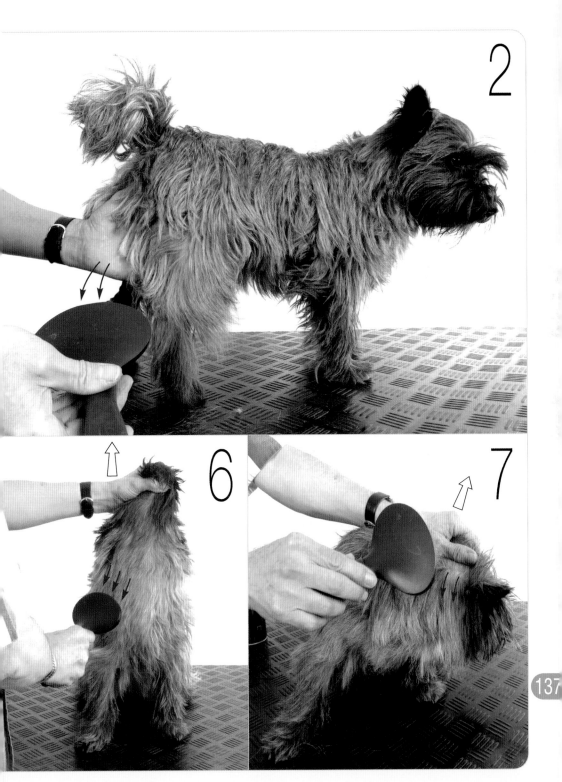

2

6

7

continued overleaf ▶

Finishing

1: Brush and comb the muzzle and carefully comb the whiskers and eyebrows.

2: Turn the dog round, raise the front leg and brush under the leg and along the body.

3: Taking a secure grip of the back leg over the body and brush around the hind quarters, back and rump.

4: Use a comb all over the body to impart the finishing touches, paying attention to friction areas under the legs, behind the ears and under the tail.

5: The finished dog – tidy and ready for anything!

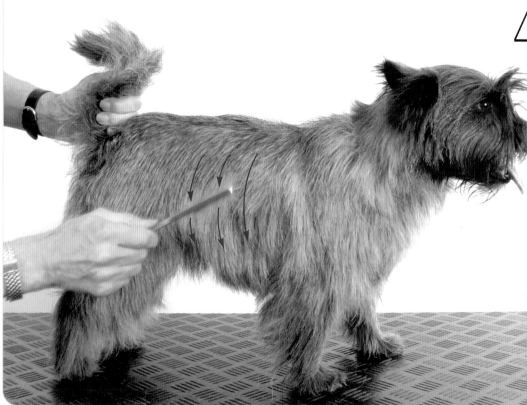

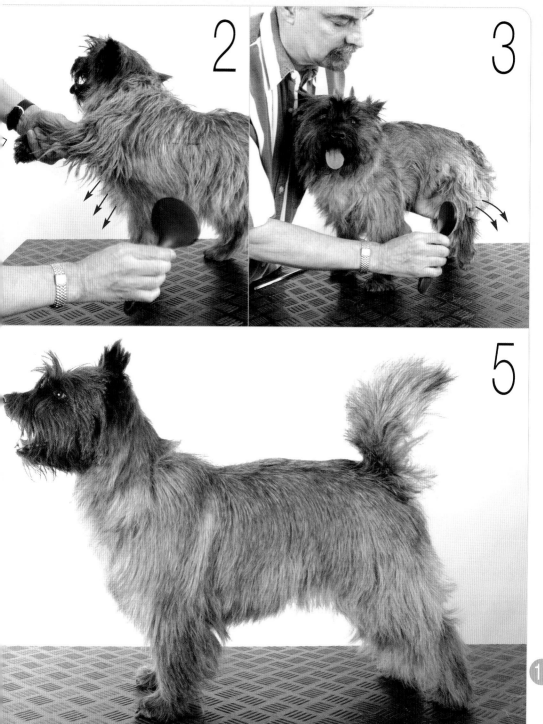

Professional Parlour Tips

Caring Grooming For Older Dogs

• Like humans, dogs experience physical changes as they get older. Their bodies function less efficiently and they are sometimes prone to diseases which can affect coat growth – for example, diabetes, Addison's disease and Cushing's disease.

Both can have dramatic effects on the dog's body, its coat and often make the dog appear a little bloated. Once diagnosed, however, they can easily be stabilised with appropriate drugs.

Also with age come problems with limb and joint soreness or arthritis which means that, if possible, it is best to groom your pet while it is lying down. The older pet will sometimes collect more sleepy matter in his or her eyes which will need daily cleaning. And with reduced amounts of exercise, the nails will often need more frequent attention to keep the foot comfortable. Look out for cracked pads too, which small amounts of paw balm or wax will help to soothe.

Coats can become thinner with age and the quality of the skin can change becoming significantly dryer and more likely to shed surface skin cells. If this happens, a more nourishing

Above: *Be aware that a dog's grooming and care needs will change as it grows older.*

shampoo and conditioner may be the answer. If this does not seem to improve the situation, one of the veterinary shampoos may be more suitable. And shampooing will usually need to be done on a more frequent basis to obtain optimum benefit. The interval between shampoos will vary from weekly to monthly depending on the nature of the individual case and on the advice of the shampoo manufacturer and your vet.

Some breeds, like Poodles, Bichons, Yorkies and Schnauzers, seem to be susceptible as they age to growing warts or small skin eruptions which you obviously need to avoid while grooming. There is often an area around the wart which has a tendency to produce an extremely waxy

discharge which coats the immediately surrounding hair. This may eventually form a scab over the wart. It is really better to keep this hair short. Neatly trim it with scissors, thereby allowing the maximum amount of fresh air to circulate around the wart which helps to keep it cleaner and dryer. Warts seldom disappear of their own accord, and any removal treatment can only be applied in areas where the dog cannot lick or otherwise get access to it with its mouth. If they become troublesome or unsightly, warts can be surgically removed by a veterinarian.

There are many supplements, available at your local pet store, which can be either added to the food or given in the form of chewsticks or tablets which will help to improve the mobility of dogs with arthritis or joint problems. The main components of almost every dog joint or arthritis-prevention supplement are glucosamine and chondroitin, which are essential to the forming of healthy joint cartilage and synovial fluid.

Common Problems Associated With Grooming

• Over the years that I have been practising as a professional dog groomer,

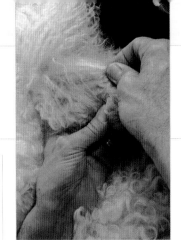

...ave encountered various little ...oblems that commonly arise ...hen people are learning to ...oom their pets at home. I ...tline four of the most common ...re, and useful remedies to ...al with them.

...ush burn

This occurs when people are ... little too enthusiastic or even ...ggressive with a slicker or pin ...ush in their desire to do a ...od job. The dog may end up ...th red lines on the skin as a ...sult of the pins of the brush ...raping it too vigorously. ...eedless to say, as soon as you ...e aware of this problem, you ...ould stop work in that ...mediate area. If severe, this ...raping can lead to a skin ...itation. Monitor the area for a ...hile – an hour or two. If it still ...oks very red and angry after ...at time, seek veterinary ...tention. But it may settle down ...y itself if the irritation is not too ...vere.

Practise brushing on the ...derside of your arm to feel the ...rrect amount of pressure and ...e of stroke that is suitable for ...ch brush that you use. It ...ould apply a gentle pressure ... the coat and then pull or slide ...sily away through the hair.

...ats and tangles

...You may find yourself in a ...uation where you have tried

Above: *With care, mats can be broken down and brushed out. But very neglected coats may need to be clipped.*

unsuccessfully to brush away or detangle a mat but still have most of it in place. It is possible with care to split the offending area into smaller sections with a mat breaker or small pair of scissors and these smaller clumps can then be brushed out individually.

If using scissors, hold the skin firmly at the root of the mat and, working away from the body, split the mat lengthwise into small strands for further brushing out. Likewise, if using a mat breaker, hold the base of the mat without pulling on the dog's skin, and use as directed on the product's packaging.

Clipper rash or burn

• This is caused when the blade used on the clipper is set too short with regard to the sensitivity of the individual dog's skin. It does not actually cause a burn, but it does certainly cause an irritation or tickle which the dog will then worry at – either

by scratching the area if it can reach it, rubbing the area along a carpet or sofa to relieve the itch, or by nibbling at it. All of these things usually end up making what was a small irritation into a much bigger wound which of course takes longer to heal. As long as the irritation is minor, applying calamine lotion may help to calm it down. Otherwise a little coating of Vaseline helps to seal the area but it is messier. If the irritation does not start to clear up after a day or so, seek veterinary attention.

Minor nicks or cuts

• Should you have the misfortune to cut or nick a dog with either scissors or clippers, try not to panic as this will only aggravate both you and the dog. Assess the situation: where is the wound, how deep is it, etc? No matter where the wound is, try to apply pressure at the base of it to stop the flow of blood – e.g. if it's an ear tip, press just below the wound and hold tight for ten minutes or so, then carefully relax the pressure and see whether the bleeding has stopped of its own accord. If the wound is more severe and to a leg, consider applying a tourniquet for a short while and then wrapping the wound with a pressure bandage until you can reach a vet.

continued overleaf ▶

Professional Parlour Tips

Things Not To Do When Grooming

• Certainly one of the biggest don'ts is never bathe a heavily tangled dog as the shampooing process will only make the matting become tighter and retain shampoo residue. Both can cause irritation – as the mats get tighter they will pull on the skin and the shampoo residue may cause an adverse skin reaction. Slight tangling may be removed using a good shampoo and conditioner followed by a thorough dry, but heavy tangling and matting requires proper brushing through or even professional help before bathing should be attempted.

Above: If your dog's coat is heavily matted and tangled, **do not bath it**. You will only make a bad situation even worse.

Don't leave it too long between your grooming sessions, as the longer you leave it, the more work will have to be put in by you and your dog to get a decent result. Establish a routine and leave yourself sufficient time to complete it in a relaxed state of mind: things never work out when you try to rush them, and tempers are like to get frayed.

Is My Dog Good Enough If I Want To Show It?

• The term "dog show" generally refers to a breed competition, in which the dogs are judged on the basis of appearance, physique, size and shape, showmanship and temperament, according to the breed standard: i.e. a description of a perfect specimen of the breed as laid down by a regulatory authority such as the Kennel Club. A standard is a very detailed description, discussing everything from the nose, its shape and colour, to the size and position of the tail, how the dog moves and its general expression. And it includes a definition of the dog's purpose or function, which is generally indicated by the group classification into which it falls: i.e. hound, terrier, gundog, toy

dog etc. A deviation from the standard is considered a fault. Thus, a fault could be physical – such as having legs which are too long – or relate to an incorrect temperament, and such faults can be assessed during a brief examination at a show by an experienced judge. The standard serves as a guide for judges and breeders alike, and a copy can be obtained from your national Kennel Club.

Dog showing is quite an involved sport, and there are many different levels of showing. The highest is the Championship Show, such as Crufts. Below this comes the Open Show, then the Members Limited Show, and lastly the Exemption or fun show at which serious show dogs cannot compete, thereby giving people new to showing a chance. If you want to show your dog in a serious or slightly serious way apart from at the Exemption shows (where you have pedigree classes and also classes for crossbreeds and mixed breeds), it will have to be a pedigree dog registered at your national Kennel Club and will need a greater or lesser amount of ringcraft training depending on how much initial training you have put in yourself.

The trainers at a local ringcraft training club will be able to advise you if your pet is good enough to show and how find more information about shows. Their phone numbers can be usually be obtained via the Kennel Club, and they certainly do help with socialisation and basic training of young dogs as they train you to train your dog – plus it can be a fun night out for you too.

Many a quality dog sold as a pet has ended up as a champion, though it always needs training and the right presentation, typical for its respective breed. I hope that by reading this book you will have found out more about making your own dog look its best and that one day I might see you both on the winner's podium!

The Need For Professional Grooming

Hopefully, after reading this book, you will be able to do a large amount of maintenance grooming yourself – and enjoy the process. But there are times when most of the coated breeds need professional attention. Some people will be able and want to bathe and trim their dogs at home, but this can be a messy business, and some will want the convenience of a professional doing the work. The choice is yours.

If you are looking for a reputable groomer, one of the

Above: *Professional groomers have specialist knowledge of how to deal with all types of coat. Owners of high-maintenance breeds often seek the help of a professional to supplement their home grooming.*

best sources is word of mouth recommendation. Alternatively you may want to contact your local veterinary practice and ask them to advise you. In the UK you can contact the Pet Care Trust on 01234 273 933: this is the governing body of the licensed dog groomers' association and education board. They hold a databank of qualified groomers, i.e. those who have passed the City & Guilds qualification in grooming, showing that they have the necessary theory and practical knowledge to trim safely and to high standards. Being a qualified groomer involves more than just cutting a dog's hair. The qualified groomer should have a good knowledge of health and safety, hair growth and structure,

correct trimming techniques, suitable products such as shampoos for the optimum benefit of the pet, and how to work in a safe environment.

Most breeds that have to be trimmed, clipped or stripped will need this doing on a regular four-, six-, eight- or 12-week basis depending on the breed, the rate of coat growth, the owner's requirements and how much maintenance grooming is done at home. Breeds including the Bichons, the Poodles, most clipped terriers and spaniels will usually benefit from the services of a professional groomer plus some home maintenance – unless you want to do it all at home yourself. Hopefully yours will be a happy, well-cared-for dog – and it's much easier to love a clean, well-groomed pet.

Index

Page numbers appearing in **bold** type indicate the main reference to a subject. Page numbers in *italics* refer to captions to illustrations.

Picture Credits Unless otherwise credited here, all the photographs reproduced in this book were taken for Interpet Publishing by Mark Burch.
Bayer HealthCare: 18, 22, 23 (all).
Jane Burton, Warren Photographic: *7* top right, *7* top inset, *7* upper centre inset, *9*, *13*, *17*, *25* bottom, *26*, *33*, *45* top right, *76-7*, *90*, *90-1*, *92* bottom, *98-9*, *99* (all three), *108-9*, *109* (all three); *117* top right, *124-5*, *125* top, *133* centre right, *133* bottom.
Crestock.com: Eric Isselée: *117* bottom right.
Dreamstime.com: Eric Isselée: *77* top right.
Fotolia.com: Callalloo Canis: *11* bottom. Eric Isselée: *14*, *117* top left. Elliot Westacott: *15* bottom right.
Interpet Archive: *16*, *21*, *25* top, *125* centre right.

iStockphoto.com: Aldra: *42*. Bojan Fatur: *142*. Eric Isselée: *24* bottom, *46*, *78* bottom right. Oliver Sun Kim: *19* top. Eric Lam: *116-7*, *119* centre right. Greg Nicholas: *45* bottom inset, *143*. Anna Utekhina: *24* top.
Merial Animal Health Ltd: *20* (lice and mites).
Shutterstock.com: WilleeCole: *4*. Phil Date: *91* top right. Svetlana Gladkova: *15* top. Eric Isselée: *83* top left, *83* bottom right, *91* bottom right, *132*, *133* top left. Petr Jilek: *27* bottom right. Kudrashka-a: *43*. Vladislav Lebedinski: *82-3*, *84* bottom. Dina Magnat: *126* bottom. Dariusz Majgier: *19* bottom. Guðjón Eyjólfur Ólafsson: *27* top. Zoltan Pataki: *29* top right. Phase4Photography: *11* top. Skeletoriad: *77* top left. Magdalena Szachowska: *83* top right. Jan de Wild: *29* top left. Monika Wisniewska: *15* bottom left.